# the Morality Maze

## What is right, and why?

### by Ward Patterson

You may obtain a 64-page leader's guide to accompany this paperback. Order number 41011 from Standard Publishing or your local supplier.

A Division of Standard Publishing
Cincinnati, Ohio 45231
No. 41010

# TABLE OF CONTENTS

Unless otherwise noted, Scripture quotations are from the New American Standard Bible, © The Lockman Foundation 1971, and are used by permission. Occasionally quoted is the New English Bible (NEB), © The Delegates of the Oxford University Press and the Syndics of the Cambridge University Press, 1961, 1970.

Library of Congress Cataloging in Publication Data
Patterson, Ward.
   The morality maze.

   1. Christian ethics. 2. Ethics. I. Title.
BJ1251.P32          241          81-14539
ISBN 0-87239-478-6                     AACR2

Printed in U.S.A.                          1982

# MORAL
# PERSPECTIVES

*Please read 1 Thessalonians 4:1-12; 5:14-24*

God created things which had free will. That means creatures which can go either wrong or right. Some people think they can imagine a creature which was free but had no possibility of going wrong; I cannot.[1]

This is a book about what the philosopher calls ethics, the theologian calls morals, the educator calls values, the man-on-the-street calls goodness, and the Bible calls righteousness. It is a book about knowing the right and doing the right.

Ever since Adam and Eve disobeyed God at the tree of the knowledge of good and evil, mankind has been struggling to define the good and do the right. The quest for standards of right conduct is distinctly a human endeavor. Man alone thinks in terms of ought's and why's.

---

1. Reprinted with permission of Macmillan Publishing Co., Inc., from *Mere Christianity* by C. S. Lewis. Copyright 1943, 1945, 1952 by Macmillan Publishing Co., Inc. Copyrights renewed.

He asks himself whether or not there are universal standards of right conduct that apply to all men everywhere. He notes that all people everywhere have a sense that some things are right and others are wrong, even though they may in fact disagree about which are which. He ponders the nature of his conscience, the policeman within him. He asks whether moral conduct is mandated by God or merely the product of parental training and social convention.

## The Age of Permissiveness

We live in an age of permissiveness, a time of the "new morality." Constraints have fallen and moral consensus has vanished. Many contemporary theologians and philosophers assert that man has "come of age" and that he has outgrown the outdated Judeo-Christian morality of the Bible.

## The Signs of the Times

Yet others of us look about and shudder at the deadly fallout of this new-age morality. We see a world that has lost its moral moorings. A president and a pope are wounded by would-be assassins. The Abscam investigations convict legislators of taking bribes to influence governmental action. Atlanta and the nation weep with each day's rising body count of innocent black children murdered on its streets. People buy guns for self-protection at an unprecedented rate. California expects to issue about one million tear-gas licenses this year to citizens worried about self-protection. Elderly people fear to go out and fear for their lives and property when they are at home. Crime has spread to the country from the cities. The open-door policy of old no longer is practiced in small towns. Crimes are increasingly random, irrational, and brutal.

A murder is committed in the United States every twenty-four minutes, a rape every seven minutes, a house burglary every ten seconds. Harry Scarr, the former director of the Bureau of Justice, predicts that within four or five years every household in the United States will be hit by crime.

While at virtually the same time his court was ruling that the Ten Commandments could not legally be displayed in Kentucky schools, Chief Justice of the U.S. Supreme Court, Warren E. Burger, lamented a "reign of terror" that is engulfing our nation. In an address to the American Bar Association, he said, "Today we are approaching the status of an impotent society—whose capability of maintaining elementary security on the streets, in schools, and in the homes of our people is in doubt." Further, he said, the rate of "day-by-day terrorism in almost any large city exceeds the casualties of all the reported international terrorists in any given year. . . . Why do we show such indignation over alien terrorists and such tolerance for the domestic variety?"

The schools have become dangerous battlegrounds. In 1979, one hundred ten thousand teachers, one of every twenty, reported being attacked by a student. One out of every eight high-school teachers reports a hesitation to confront students because of fear.

Over a six-year period the Los Angeles County Schools lost nearly one hundred million dollars because of school muggings, lawsuits, theft, and vandalism. Things have gotten so bad that the Attorney General of the State of California has brought suit against the mayor of Los Angeles, the city council, the chief of police, and the board of trustees of the school district for their inability to provide safe places for student education.

Chief Gates, of the Los Angeles police force, said,

We've lost a whole generation. Totally lost. No self-discipline. Total indulgence. Drugs. Lack of respect for the law. Lack of respect for values. A whole generation thumbed its nose at everything that was held sacred in the country. America has to take a look at its heart and its soul.[2]

"Ripping off" has become a national pastime. Lying has been dignified by the term "disinformation." Cheating is taken for granted. A fast-growing business in university towns is the ghostwriting of term papers, which are purchased and submitted as student work. Some are written by professors themselves. Half the colleges of the Pacific-10 Conference are put on probation for dealing with falsified college transcripts. If this is what student's are learning in college, is it any wonder that deception and dishonesty are becoming more and more common in our society?

The Internal Revenue Service estimates that deceptive practices cause the Treasury Department a loss of eighteen billion dollars a year. An employee of a prestigious Wall Street investment firm is indicted for leaking information of mergers in such a way as to reap great profits. Janet Cooke is forced to return the Pulitzer Prize when it is learned that her winning story is fabricated. Rosie Ruiz is declared the winner of the Boston Marathon, only to be disqualified because it is alleged she did not run the complete race. And to top it all off, a leading Christian magazine drops its listing of the "100 Largest Sunday Schools" because churches are falsifying their reports.

Frank Trippett, writing in *Time* magazine, suggests the following reasons for the increase in deception that seems to pervade our times:

> The general relaxation of moral codes is doubtless one. Another is the steadily growing pressure for personal achievement in an increasingly competitive world. The incentive to cheat is heightened

by the fact that society is more and more an aggregate of strangers dealing impersonally with one another. Finally, there is the snowballing impression that everybody must be cheating.[3]

Suicide is now the third leading cause of death among young people between the ages of fifteen and nineteen. Many of these are coming from affluent families. The North Shore area of Chicago, with a mean annual income of sixty thousand dollars, had twenty-eight suicides in a seventeen-month period. A British magazine, *Now!*, is publishing a do-it-yourself guide to suicide, a ten-thousand-word pamphlet called *A Guide to Self-Deliverance,* which gives instructions on five recommended methods, complete with dosages and easy-to-follow instructions. Jo Roman is the subject of a TV documentary as she throws a party for her friends and then, with their full knowledge, quietly commits suicide in the next room.

Last year more than a million teen-age girls, one out of every ten, got pregnant. Over one-third of these had abortions. According to a recent report, nearly fifty percent of American girls between fifteen and nineteen have had premarital sex. Venereal disease is at epidemic proportions. Abortion has become the most frequently performed operation in America. There have been over nine and a half million abortions since they were first legalized in the United States.

Drunkenness is a national scandal. One out of every eleven people who drink is an alcoholic. There are at least ten million alcoholics in America. Alcohol costs business, industry, government, and the military over ten billion dollars annually in lost hours of work, and it costs another three billion dollars in property damage and medical costs. It is involved in at least half the fatal automobile

3. *Time,* October 20, 1980, p. 106.

accidents each year, thus accounting for over twenty-five thousand deaths annually.

America's divorce rate is the highest in the world. Nearly forty percent of U.S. marriages end in divorce, the majority during the first two years of marriage. One out of every six children will spend at least two years in a single-parent home.

The incidence of rape has doubled within the past decade. Though it is often an unreported crime, approximately seventy thousand cases are reported annually.

Pornography, grossing each year more than four billion dollars, has become well established in our business districts. Child abuse and incest are on the rise.

There seems no end to it all. A nine-year-old boy commits a bank robbery in New York City. Companies dump toxic wastes surreptitiously in streams, poisoning underground water supplies. Scientists falsify data, doctors do unnecessary operations, and auto mechanics charge for undone or unnecessary repairs.

In addition to these areas of traditional moral concern, mankind is entering a "brave new world" of genetic engineering, cloning, artificial insemination, surrogate mothers, and test-tube babies. A new study, bioethics, has made its appearance as we have begun to grapple with the moral implications of recent scientific discoveries.

In the midst of all this, we seek to find our way toward truth, goodness, righteousness, honesty, and respect. This book is written with the conviction that the Bible and the Bible alone offers guidance through the labyrinth of conflicting values that perplex us today. Our concern will be to look at two areas: (1) Ethical Alternatives and (2) Biblical Imperatives.

# Section 1:
# *ETHICAL ALTERNATIVES*

# MORAL
# PERPLEXITIES

*Please read Exodus 20:1-17;
Deuteronomy 6:4-7; 10:12, 13; 11:26-28; 12:8.*

God's laws are usually general in nature, and require honest and sincere application to the *particular* situations of our lives. . . . This is part of the very genius of the Bible. Here in one small volume, carried in one hand or pocket, are all the laws needed to govern the conduct of all peoples of all times! How is this possible? It is possible because the laws are mostly so general that they transcend cultural differences, and can be given relevant applications from culture to culture, from age to age.[1]

"He shouldn't have. . . ." "We ought to. . . ." "It was wrong to. . . ." We use such language daily. We seem to assume that others understand us, that there is a common standard of good that all thinking people accept. We communicate our judgment, make our case, pronounce our opinion, and set the course of our action on

---

1. Quotation from *His Way*, Jack Cottrell, p. 9, © 1980. The Standard Publishing Company, Cincinnati, Ohio. Division of Standex International Corporation. Used by permission.

the basis of this assumed ground of human conduct.

Where that sense of rightness came from does not ordinarily concern us. If we say, "It was wrong to lie about Watergate," we do not add some explanatory statement like "because the Bible says lying is wrong" or possibly "because my mother told me that lying is wrong." We are not much bothered by the origin of the peculiarly human quality of moral judgment that we exercise so casually each day. Yet that which we treat so casually is far from simple.

## Questions Everywhere

Questions of morality and ethics touch every aspect of human behavior. Walking my dog may seem a simple action without great social or moral implications. But without realizing it I begin to make decisions of an ethical nature. Do I have a responsibility to the shrubbery, flowers, and legs of my neighbors as well as to my Saint Bernard? I call her Saint Helens, but she is not really destructive—just as big as a mountain. I have heard that there may be a law in our town that all dogs and owners must be on leashes when they go outside. But Mrs. Farnsworth, my neighbor, never puts her dog on a leash. And poodles are such nervous dogs. My neighbors might laugh if they saw me being dragged down the street by Saint Helens. How about a muzzle? Saint Helens has, on occasion, nipped playfully at the heels of a jogger or two. But a muzzle would give the wrong impression about Saint Helens. People might think she is vicious. How often should I walk Saint Helens? How long should I walk her? How far is right? And if I cannot walk Saint Helens properly in my crowded asphalt neighborhood and with my crowded hectic schedule, ought I to trade her in on a chihuahua?

"Hardly the stuff of great ethical drama," you say. But it is clear that for every choice I make, for every behavior, for every proposed action, there is likely to be a wealth of ethical considerations. Some of these considerations may be codified into law in order to bring regularity and maximum social responsibility into our actions. Leash and muzzle laws are common, and New York City not long ago decreed that pet owners are responsible to pick up the leavings of pets that are not properly city-broken. Little pails and shovels have become the common identifying symbols of Central Park dog lovers.

Laws move some ethical questions from the realm of personal decision to the area of prescribed behavior. But the debate goes on as to whether a law is a good one, whether it really corrects the problem, whether it creates more bad than good, and whether it ought to be rigidly enforced and scrupulously obeyed.

## The Lost Consensus

In many areas of judgment we talk and act as if there were commonly accepted standards of right behavior, of fair play, of truth and honesty, of right and wrong, that all accept. But we have a vague feeling that with each passing day something is being chipped away from the moral foundations that undergird the thinking of our nation.

Ten years ago William Barclay commented during some television interviews,

> But thirty years ago no one ever really questioned the Christian ethic. Thirty years ago no one ever doubted that divorce was disgraceful; that illegitimate babies were a disaster; that chastity was a good thing; that an honest day's work was part of the duty of any respectable and responsible man; that honesty ought to be part of life. But today, for the first time in history, the whole Christian ethic is under attack.[2]

2. William Barclay, *Ethics in a Permissive Society* (Harper & Row, Publishers, Inc. 1972), p. 13.

There are many who would say that our ill-ease with modern morality is unwarranted. This loss of the Christian moral consensus in our country is heralded by them as a great leap forward. As one college sophomore wrote to his school newspaper,

> The current breakdown in Judeo-Christian morality is due to the fact that it has outlived its usefulness. The time has come for the next step in the religious-ethical evolution of mankind. We are entering a new Age, a new stage in our unfoldment as potential gods.

Man, it is claimed, has "come of age" in that he has now come to the place where he can derive his own principles of conduct without reference to an outside authority like God. As a college junior put it in another letter to his college newspaper,

> I perceive the reason for this falling away to be a gradual maturation of the American people—they no longer take very seriously a philosophy that does no more than appeal to authority to justify its moral dogma. To remedy the so-called moral deterioration of America (if it in fact exists), we do not need a resurgence of Judeo-Christian morality, for its dogma cannot be effective with an intellectually mature person. If anything, what is needed is a complete rejection of this morality and a replacement of it with a rational, human morality so that persons will choose not to, for example, steal, because they understand it is undesirable, not because it is labeled for them by someone else as "wrong."

These college young people share a common optimism as to the ability of man to create his own moral values apart from God. There are many of us who look at history and the contemporary moral morass and seriously question their optimism. We wonder just how new this emphasis on individual, man-centered morality actually is.

The college sophomore I quoted earlier went on in his letter,

> In astrological terms we are beginning the Age of Aquarius, an age of freedom and enlightenment when man realizes his identity with God instead of needing a mediator such as Jesus Christ. A manifesto of Aquarian morality published by the Ordo Templi Orientis states, "There is no god but man. Man has the right to live by his own law—to live, to work, to play, to rest as he will—to die when and how he will. Man has the right to eat what he will, to move as he will on the face of the earth. Man has the right to think what he will, to speak, to write, to draw, to paint, to carve, to etch, to mold, to build as he will, to dress as he will. Man has the right to love as he will—when, where and with whom he will. Man has the right to kill those who would thwart these rights." When the majority accepts and follows these inherent birthrights of man, he will surely enter the Golden Age.

## New Age Morality

There is nothing particularly new about a morality governed only by the desires of the individual man and his right to do whatever he pleases without regard for anyone but himself. It is the oldest paganism in the world. It is the prescription for the death of a civilization. It is the law of the jungle. It is worse than that—for even jungle predators exercise self-control.

This "new-age" morality focuses on rights, not responsibilities. It is symptomatic of the "Me-Decade," the

"Age of Narcissism," that we are living through. Where, in this new-age morality, is place for taking into account the rights of others not to be exploited by our wills, not to be lied to for our selfish purposes, not to be used for our benefit, not to be manipulated for our pleasure, not to be degraded for our personal enjoyment?

The clincher of the letter has even more shocking implications: "Man has the right to kill those who would thwart these rights." This Aquarian morality, this great step forward in religious-ethical evolution, gives us the right to *kill* anyone who stands in the way of our doing whatever we please! If an employer should be so non-Aquarian as to fire me because I do not choose to work according to his wishes, then, of course, I have a perfect moral right to plant a bomb in his office and blow him to pieces. If the mayor intrudes on my right to live where I will by preventing me from building my house on public land, I have a perfect right to blow his head off. What a wonderful Golden Age, with its Aquarian morality to take the place of the outmoded Judeo-Christian morality of responsibility, love, and respect!

## Old Age Paganism

Paul's words to the pagans of his century apply equally well to the pagans of our day, "Their wits are beclouded, they are strangers to the life that is in God, because ignorance prevails among them and their minds have grown hard as stone. Dead to all feeling, they have abandoned themselves to vice, and stop at nothing to satisfy their foul desires" (Ephesians 4:18, 19 NEB).

William Barclay, commenting on the ancient pagans, noted that they were unfeeling and insensitive. Their hearts were as if petrified as they looked only at what prospered and pleased them. They abandoned themselves to unclean conduct, giving in to insatiable lust for every desire of their hearts. They were incapable of bearing the pain of discipline. They were arrogant in their greediness and would sacrifice a neighbor for their own desires. They were so much at the mercy of their desires that they did not care whose life was injured and whose innocence was destroyed in the satisfaction of those desires.

> So long as self is at the center of things, so long as our feelings, our prestige, are the only things that matter, this oneness (peace) can never fully exist. It can only exist when we cease to make self the center of things and when we think more of others than we do of ourselves. Self kills peace. In a society where self predominates, men cannot be other than a disintegrated collection of individualistic warring units. But when self dies and Christ springs to life within our hearts, then there comes the peace, the oneness, the togetherness, which is the great hallmark of the true Church.[3]

We might suppose that these ideas of college young people were only the random, untypical fancies of immature minds, but this is unfortunately not the case. These young people are expressing the current consensus of countless students and college professors. They are reflecting the predominant drift of our educational institutions, our media, and our society at large. We have experienced a "great leap backward" to the morality described in the book of Judges: "In those days there was no king in Israel; every man did what was right in his own eyes" (Judges 17:6).

## Who Will Be King?

One of the great questions of ethics and morality is who will be king. God? Self? Society? Physical nature? No

3. From *THE LETTERS TO THE GALATIANS AND EPHESIANS,* Translated with Introductions and Interpretations by William Barclay. First published by The Saint Andrew Press. Published in the U.S.A. by The Westminster Press. Used by permission.

one at all? For the people of Israel this question was clearly answered by God's covenant relationship, by God's mighty works in calling them out of Egypt as a free people, and in His revelation of His law on Mount Sinai. The opening Commandment of that matchless law code made it abundantly clear who is King. God alone is the focus of life and actions. He is central to an understanding of iniquity and righteousness. He is the judge of all. His commandments reveal the standards by which judgment is made. His name is to be honored by human conduct, His example to be imitated. Principles of human interraction grow out of relationship with God.

C. S. Lewis wrote, as appears in *Mere Christianity:*

> Morality, then, seems to be concerned with three things. Firstly, with fair play and harmony between individuals. Secondly, with what might be called tidying up or harmonizing the things inside each individual. Thirdly, with the general purpose of human life as a whole: what man was made for: what course the whole fleet ought to be on: what tune the conductor of the band wants it to play.[4]

These elements parallel, in reverse order, the law as summed up by Jesus, " 'Hear, O Israel; the Lord our God is one Lord; and you shall love the Lord your God with all your heart, and with all your soul, and with all your mind, and with all your strength.' The second is this, 'You shall love your neighbor as yourself' " (Mark 12:29-31). The three elements of relationship, God, self, and neighbor, are all important to morality, but God is preeminent. How could it be otherwise? He designed the universe to harmonize with His own nature.

---

4. Reprinted with permission of Macmillan Publishing Co., Inc. from *Mere Christianity* by C. S. Lewis. Copyright 1943, 1945, 1952 by Macmillan Publishing Co., Inc. Copyrights renewed.

## The Mountains of Morality

The ethical foundation-stones laid at Sinai through Moses (Exodus 20:1-17) and on a mountain in Galilee by Jesus (Matthew 5—7) have stood through thousands of years of human experience. Even those who profess to be initiating a new standard of morality must give grudging recognition to the mountain revelations of the Old and New Testaments. These divine principles will still be standing long after the "new moralities" of today have become the "old foolishness" of the past (Psalm 14:1).

How is it that moral principles, some of them first recorded over three thousand years ago, continue to exert influence today? We would not go to the ancient writings of the Egyptians for the key to modern space exploration. We would not go to the ancient practices of the Greek physicians for instructions about heart transplants. But we find ourselves inevitably drawn to this timeless book, the Bible, for instruction in that most basic of human endeavors, the art of living.

How is it that the Bible transcends time and circumstance? By giving overriding principles for the identification of right and wrong. It does not give detailed rules for every possible situation that can arise in our lives, but it does give principles to be prayerfully, intelligently, courageously, and humbly applied. The claims of the new morality notwithstanding, God's principles remain unshaken. God is on the throne of the universe whether we recognize His sovereignty or not.

# MORAL  PHILOSOPHY

*Please read Psalm 119:1-24, 97-105.*

"We can fail to act morally and still be human, but to lose the capacity to distinguish between the moral and the immoral is to lose our humanity."[1]

There are many clocks and watches throughout the United States. Some, like the one in my car, run extremely fast. Others are slow. Some have stopped, and others are broken. Others are precision instruments. But all these clocks have one thing in common. They are designed to tell time, whether they actually do it very well or not. Their relative goodness, in respect to "true time," is judged against an external standard, the standard of the Naval Observatory in Washington. That standard, in turn, is established on the basis of astronomical observation. Correct time is not determined by any man-made clock, but by the motion of the earth; and that is set and regulated by the Creator.

1. Richard L. Purtell, *Reason to Believe* (William B. Eerdmans Publishing Company). p. 94.

## Standards

Christians claim, in like manner, that some external standard is necessary against which to judge all the varieties of human conduct. Just as navigation, communication, and government would be impossible without a recognized standard of time, the Christian believes that good conduct, communication, and community cannot be established without an external standard against which all actions must be judged. Thus the Christian builds his moral world on a fixed standard, outside himself, residing in God, revealed through the Bible, valid for all men and women, throughout all time. That standard is as sure and unchanging as the God who upholds it.

The relativist, in contrast, suggests that there is no external clock. He has decided to accept every clock at face value. Whatever one clock says is just as true as whatever any other clock says. But this is a position of disharmony, confusion, and despair. He may, as an alternative, survey all the clocks he can get his hands on and find the average time from among them all. This is certainly more helpful than the individualistic approach to time. But what if he finds that another person, examining a different sample of clocks, comes up with another "true time" of his own? How are the two of them to settle their dispute about "true time"? The relativist has no solution to this unless, of course, he goes outside his system to justify his conclusion.

Relativism, subjectivisim, and individuality seem to be the watchwords of our day. Yet, somehow, absolutes seem to creep back in, even in the statement that "all things are relative." R. C. Sproul pointed out that the youth culture of the sixties lived by two conflicting mottoes: "Everybody do his thing" and "Tell it like it is." The first implied that there are no real moral absolutes and that everyone should be free to do exactly what he pleases. The second appealed to an outside standard for truth by which all people and actions ought to be judged.

In the name of freedom they wanted to throw away moral standards, and in the name of justice they wanted to invoke them.

C. S. Lewis wrote, "Whenever you find a man who says he does not believe in a real Right and Wrong, you will find the same man going back on this a moment later."[2] Scholars who say there is no such thing as right or wrong, strangely, become morally indignant when a colleague falsifies research data.

## Ethics and Morality

You may have noted that I have been using the terms *ethics* and *morality* synonymously. This is appropriate, I think, because both come from roots with the same meaning, though *ethics* comes from the Greek and *morals* comes from the Latin. The roots of both mean "custom" or "habitual mode of conduct." In English usage through the years, *morality* has tended to keep the original sense of custom and habit, conduct as it is commonly practiced in everyday-life situations. *Ethics,* however, has come to mean the formal, philosophical pursuit of general, systematic standards for evaluating human conduct in general. In a sense, ethics asked, "Why ought . . . ?" and morality asked, "What is . . . ?" These distinctions are still made in ethical discussion, but now we are more likely to speak of normative or descriptive ethics.

These two terms represent two different ways of looking at the right in human conduct. Normative ethics discusses the right—defining it, examining it, identifying it in such a way that principles can be established for application to particular situations as they arise. It is interested in what "ought" to be done. To use our clock metaphor, it seeks to establish what Naval Observatory time is. Descriptive ethics is interested in describing what people do,

2. Reprinted with permission of Macmillan Publishing Co., Inc. from *Mere Christianity* by C. S. Lewis. Copyright 1943, 1945, 1952 by Macmillan Publishing Co., Inc. Copyrights renewed.

how they really act, what they are really doing. By this approach, one would seek to establish "true time" by examining and reporting on a representative sample of clocks.

Since people generally do not live up to the standards of morality to which they give lip service, these two approaches to ethics are likely to lead to conflicting conclusions. The question, primarily, is whether there are some things that are right to do whether or not they are commonly done, or whether common practice is the best key into what is normal and right for mankind. Normative ethics examines motives, actions, and results in light of established principles. Descriptive ethics samples, surveys, and observes in search of practiced norms of human behavior. The tools of the first are revelation and reason; the tools of the latter are statistical theory and experimental method.

Normal reason tells us that there is a great gap between an "is" and an "ought." Morality by majority is no morality at all. One hundred percent of speaking people have lied, but that hardly demonstrates that lying is what people ought to do. The Bible clearly says that majority conduct is usually wrong (Matthew 7:13, 14) and that right is right whether or not anyone is practicing it. The prophets never conducted a survey to see what was the predominant opinion about moral issues before they thundered their "Thus saith the Lord!"

## Normal and Abnormal

Yet something curious has been happening in our society. Computer technology has given us the means of learning more and more about what people think and do. Particularly in the area of sexuality we have seen a huge surge of surveys and questionnaires designed to reveal what is going on in our nation in sexual matters. What has emerged has been presented as statistically normal human sexual behavior. This, of course, has some use, just as it might be helpful to know just how much the average clock deviates from Naval Observatory Time. Such information could help us to design better clocks, to make plans for "clock-correction seminars," and to be watchful for errors due to common clock frailty. But unfortunately such human statistical data has been interpreted in another way. What is statistically the most common has been interpreted as being behaviorally the most normal. It is a very short step to add the value judgment that what is uncommon is abnormal, hence undesirable.

The increased prominence of sexual research and reports has had the effect of normalizing, in the minds of many, conduct that would have been considered by previous generations as immoral. The theory goes, "If so many are doing it, how can it be considered wrong? If it is so natural for man, would it not be wrong for God to prohibit it?" Here again the Bible is out of step with current thinking. It says, "There is a way which seems right to a man, but its end is the way of death" (Proverbs 14:12). It is a fact that man is sinful and that his conduct is wicked. But while this is his common state, God calls him to a standard above his base desires and worst potentialities.

The prophets of Israel knew that the heart is desperately wicked (Jeremiah 17:9). They knew too that man has almost unlimited powers of self-rationalization and justification for his acts.

We commonly experience the same thing too. A man guilty of murder will cry out, "He deserved to die!" as if the murder were really a just response to a higher good than the preservation of life. We are incurably driven to justify our actions by appeal to rightness. Where does that urge come from? Why are we so conscious of our need to be moral? Why is it that lying alters our bodily equilibrium to the extent that it can be detected by a lie-detector? Why is the conscience so powerful that it can lead to physical and psychological disorders when violated? Why does mankind everywhere seem to have a compelling sense of oughtness?

These questions draw us to consider the source and character of man's unique moral nature. He alone of all creation asks himself, "Why?" He alone is a free moral agent. He alone examines his behavior and examines the fact that he examines it.

## The Law of Nature

It was once popular to speak about the law of nature. It was assumed that there was a universal moral law for human nature in the same way that there is a law of gravity in physical nature. C. S. Lewis wrote thus of it:

> This law was called the Law of Nature because people thought that every one knew it by nature and did not need to be taught it. They did not mean, of course, that you might not find an odd individual here and there who did not know it, just as you find a few people who are color-blind or have no ear for a tune. But taking the race as a whole, they thought that the human idea of decent behavior was obvious to every one. And I believe they were right.[3]

Those who have undercut this view have argued that there is a great diversity in what is labeled right and wrong among different peoples of the world. They see not conformity but diversity as they examine the moral codes on our planet. The Dobu Islanders of Malanasia, it is reported, define the good and successful man as the one who cheats and deceives most effectively. What has this in common with the Christian ethic that condemns cheating and treachery?

The answer, of course, is that they have something very significant in common. Both of them have a *sense of*

3. Lewis, *Mere Christianity*.

24

*right and wrong*. They disagree about the actions that should bear each label, but they both agree that there is such a thing as a good action and that it ought to be pursued at all cost. Bernard Ramm wrote,

> Wherever man is found he does have some rules, some principles, some oughts, some regulations. Human existence apart from some sort of commonly accepted regulations is impossible. In this sense there is universal moral consciousness.[4]

One scholar looks at man and sees diversity of individual moral judgments. Another looks at man and sees universal moral sensitivity. Both must try to explain where these judgments come from. Here we find ourselves in a discussion as to the source and nature of conscience.

## Conscience

One answer to the question of conscience is that it is merely the collective wisdom of the past, conveyed to the present in rules, taboos, and restrictions. These rules have no universal validity outside of the group that holds them. Right is merely that which has been called beneficial by custom. Moral rules are therefore arbitrary and matters of convention. If we were brought up in one culture, we would have its standards. If in another, we would have its standards. Who is to say that one set of standards is better than the other? Both are equally valid. The Dobu Islanders have just as much right to see treachery as good as the Christians do to see love as good.

Yet, somehow, we are reluctant to grant that the standards of one group are just as good as another. There is

---

4. Bernard L. Ramm, *The Right, the Good, and the Happy,* © 1971, p. 21; used by permission of WORD BOOKS, PUBLISHER, Waco, Texas 76796.

something wrong with our thinking when we find ourselves maintaining that the morality of the Nazis was just as good as that of groups that risked their lives to save the Jews from the gas chambers. Once we grant that we must make judgments between customs, we are forced to invoke some standard of judgment outside them.

Further, it is possible that within a culture new mores are developing. Even in primitive societies there are rebels calling for change in custom and reactionaries calling for a return to past orthodoxy. How can a society decide which customs should change and which ought to be preserved? Again appeal must be made to an oughtness from outside.

Some moral philosophers have chosen intuition as their key to man's moral sensitivity. They maintain that the principles of right and wrong are inherent in the nature of each individual and that there is little need for explanation beyond the fact that these principles of morality are the givens of common human nature. Many who have developed this philosophy have denied or ignored God's part in creating that intuitive nature. They see it as a natural property of mankind, a property for which there need be no further explanation.

The Bible has another answer to conscience. It does suggest that certain things are written by God into human nature. Paul wrote to the Romans, "For the wrath of God is revealed from heaven against all ungodliness and unrighteousness of men, who suppress the truth in unrighteousness, because that which is known about God is evident within them; for God made it evident to them" (Romans 1:18, 19). Further, he wrote, "For when Gentiles who do not have the Law do instinctively the things of the Law, these, not having the Law, are a law to themselves, in that they show the work of the Law written in their hearts, their conscience bearing witness, and their thoughts alternately accusing or else defending them" (Romans 2:14, 15).

But man's conscience, alone, is not a safe guide. It can be hardened by repeated sin (1 Timothy 4:2). A person can do wrong in all good conscience, as Paul did in persecuting Christians (Acts 23:1). The conscience is susceptible to wrong programming, as we see in the culture of our day. Like a computer, the conscience is only as accurate as the programming that goes into it. Paul wrote, "To the pure, all things are pure; but to those who are defiled and unbelieving, nothing is pure, but both their mind and their conscience are defiled" (Titus 1:15). Our minds and consciences bear the nature of sin. They need divine realignment and reprogramming (Romans 12:2).

To use our clock analogy again, the conscience is like a clock that keeps perfect time. But if it is set to the wrong hour to begin with, no matter what its mechanical accuracy, it will always display the wrong time.

The Bible answer to this is to conform the conscience to the Word of God. God's Word is to be meditated upon day and night, to be internalized through constant repetition, to be memorized and called to mind again and again. The psalmist wrote, "Thy word I have treasured in my heart, that I may not sin against Thee" (Psalm 119:11).

The Word of God has been neglected by our society. Seldom are principles of character and value taught in the schools of our young. Watching countless hours of crime, revenge, adultery, promiscuity, and violence on our TV screens, our young people have drunk in the pop morals of their relativistic society. Is it any wonder that they have adopted a philosophy of instant gratification (as promised by the TV commercials), of immediate resolution to problems (in thirty minutes or less) and passive participation in life ("to be entertained is to be")?

Biblical morality is under attack. It is under concerted, conscious, systematic attack in our creative arts, in our popular literature and music, on our TV screens, in our educational institutions, in our government, and even in our churches.

We must sound again the truths of God written by Moses over three thousand years ago, "Hear, O Israel! The Lord is our God, the Lord is one! And you shall love the Lord your God with all your heart and with all your soul and with all your might. And these words, which I am commanding you today, shall be on your heart; and you shall teach them diligently to your sons and shall talk of them when you sit in your house and when you walk by the way and when you lie down and when you rise up. And you shall bind them as a sign on your hand and they shall be as frontals on your forehead. And you shall write them on the doorposts of your house and on your gates" (Deuteronomy 6:4-9). Israel's uniqueness and her destiny lay in her conformity with the law of God. So it will be with any people. To obey God brings blessing; to disobey brings disaster.

# MORAL

# PRESUPPOSITIONS

*Please read Galatians 5:13—6:10.*

> Currently making the rounds of American college campuses is the question, "How are you going to recognize God when you get to heaven?" Answer: "By the big G on his sweatshirt." . . . But it is essential to make one basic point at the very outset: in the philosophy of life of every person without exception, someone or something is invested with the sweatshirt lettered "G."[1]

What I said at the close of the previous chapter is, of course, disputed by many today. Some argue, as did Bertrand Russel, that the Bible has had positively harmful effects on the morality of mankind. The idea of divine authority dictating human conscience grates on the sensibilities of both libertines and libertarians.

We mentioned earlier that an issue key to our discussion is who will sit on the throne; the Creator or the

---

1. Reprinted with permission from *CHRISTIANITY FOR THE TOUGH MINDED* by John Warwick Montgomery, published and copyright 1973, Bethany Fellowship, Inc., Minneapolis, Minnesota 55438.

created. This question lay at the heart of man's first disobedience in the Garden of Eden. Man wanted autonomy, independence, free rein to rely on his own judgments. This was the essence of his rebellion. He overstepped God's directives and did his own thing. He has been continuing this course ever since. The New Testament calls this "the boastful pride of life" (1 John 2:16). God gave man freedom in order that he might voluntarily choose God's good ways, but he has used that freedom to choose his own ways apart from God. The whole Bible is an account of God's design to bring man back to proper understanding of and participation in the freedom of obedience and the joy of divine relationship.

## Starting Points

One approach to ethics is God-centered. It is revelational (religious, divine, metaphysical) and builds its ethical structure on the nature, the will, the way, and the Word of God. The other is man-centered. It emphasizes the rational (secular, human, physical) and attempts to build its ethical structure on reason, scientific observation, and experience. The differing understanding that these two views represent leads to radically different conclusions as to human morality. Basic to these views are their differing beliefs about God and the nature of man.

The Christian revelational view holds, among other things, that God exists, that He has a will for all mankind, that He has revealed that will in the Bible, and that God has identified in that Bible certain actions that are inherently right or wrong. It holds that eternal consequence is attached to the decisions man makes in regard to God's commandments and that God is in a dynamic relationship with man in order that he may in fact be able to do the good he recognizes and desires to do. It offers a way of forgiveness, through Christ, that brings cleansing from guilt and gives hope of eternal life.

"I HAVE ONE REGRET. HE DID IT HIS WAY."

The rational view, by contrast, regards the universe as self-existent and not divinely created. The starting point for the rationalist is man, not God. The rationalist looks within human experience for the key into the good. Man alone is the creator of whatever ethical structure exists. Reason, unaided from without, is sufficient to illuminate the right. The rationalist is interested in immediate, physically-observable consequences, not eternal spiritual outcomes. His standard of good is likely to be pleasure, fulfillment, survival, power, self-actualization, or harmony. He is confident that his mind can reveal all that can be known about reality, ethics included. Man's only relationship is with the material universe, of which he himself is a contingent part.

One of the clearest and most helpful books I have seen in tracing the logical progression of philosophies that have enthroned man is James W. Sire's book, *The Universe Next Door*. I am deeply indebted to his insight into contemporary world views, much of which I will summarize in the following sections.

If man rules God out of his equation for the examination of right and wrong, what does he have left upon which to build his ethical theory? He has the physical world of matter which, for all its complexity, reveals little about right and wrong. You are not likely to learn that you should love your wife from studying sunsets or that you should not murder by studying the mating habits of the praying mantis. Nature, in this sense, is mute.

Man himself is a part of nature. He is a biological animal, a chemical machine, a piece of living matter. Perhaps he himself holds the key to his own nature, to his own purpose, to his own destiny. If a thinker has excluded God, his approach then is the study of nature as it exists in this world, and human nature in particular. Thus it may properly be called naturalism. It has become the predominant world view of our time, at least among those who do not look to God for insight into truth.

## Deism

The shift toward human rationality as opposed to divine revelation began to occur at the end of the Middle Ages. Thinkers, abandoning the previous focus on theology, gave their attention to observation of the universe. Science was born. Human reason became more and more exalted as it unlocked room after room of the observable workings of nature. Gradually there grew the conviction that human reason was capable of knowing, without assistance from outside, all there is to know about reality. The universe was fascinating, like a great clock with interconnected systems.

The first scientists kept God on the throne, but they removed the throne room from the world. God became, to them, the clockmaker who designed and built the whole complex machine of the universe. But now He was no longer involved with its operation. God was a first cause, but not personally and intimately involved in the affairs of man. This became the position known as deism.

To the deist, nature was uniform and predictable. Miracles were impossible, for everything now moved forward without the intervention of God. Man's only way of knowing God was to study the universe.

The universe, the deists said, reveals what is normal. What is normal, what is a regular part of nature, is what was intended to be. What was intended to be is right.

While the deists hung onto God as first cause, their presuppositions severely undercut any grounding in God. What had begun as a *wholesome emphasis* on reason soon became a *total reliance* on it for the whole of truth.

## Naturalism

Deism did not last long as a world view, for it contained the seeds of its own demise. Those who were the intellectual descendants of the deists insisted that there was no basis even for the God of creation. Matter only was eternal. Physical nature was uniform. Divine intervention in the affairs of the world was ruled out. Man was a machine, a combination of chemical and physical properties that man would eventually understand by means of more observation and experimentation.

These first naturalists followed the dictates of their belief system to its logical conclusion as far as God was concerned. But they did not follow them to the logical conclusion as far as man was concerned. They believed that man was not qualitatively different from any other physical object, yet they held out for man's value, his uniqueness, his importance in the scheme of things. He was valuable because of what he was able to accomplish, what he was able to learn, and what he was able to make. He was remarkable for his sense of right and wrong. Yet these naturalists could see nothing eternal in man. Since he was only matter, death was extinction. Whatever values there were, man created; but these were real values while they lasted.

## Humanism

Secular humanism takes up these views of the naturalists. Since it is virtually the religion of our educational institutions and the accepted theology of our government, we ought to give careful attention to the beliefs of humanism. The *Humanist Manifesto II* states, "We find insufficient evidence for belief in the existence of a supernatural; it is either meaningless or irrelevant to the question of the survival and fulfillment of the human race. As non-theists, we begin with humans not God, nature not deity."[2] Religion is seen as an influence inhibiting man's realization of his full potential. There is no divine purpose to life; there is no divine providence in human affairs. "While there is much that we do not know, humans are responsible for what we are or will become. No

2. Reprinted from *Humanist Manifestos I and II,* ed. by Paul Kurtz, Prometheus Books, Buffalo, N.Y., 1973, with permission of the publisher, p. 16.

deity will save us; we must save ourselves.''[3] Mankind is viewed as the product of natural evolutionary forces. There is no life after death. The only continuity is the effect we have on the lives of others.

Humanists affirm ''that moral values derive their source from human experience.''[4] The good is to be found and experienced only in the here and now. Human reason and critical intelligence offer the only key to the solving of human problems.

Humanists believe in the maximization of individual autonomy and self-realization. As to sexuality, the humanist believes that ''short of harming others or compelling them to do likewise, individuals should be permitted to express their sexual proclivities and pursue their life-styles as they desire.''[5] The humanist believes in the right of suicide and euthanasia. People are more important than rules and regulations. Society's duty is to encourage a pluralistic, political, religious, and moral climate. Governments exist primarily to increase the quality of life for their citizens. Humanists, because of their desire to draw people together, advocate a world government.

Technology, to the humanist, is the key to human progress and development. The humanist ''would resist any moves to censor basic scientific research on moral, political, or social grounds.''[6] The humanist's ultimate commitment is not to God but to man. ''At the present juncture of history, commitment to all humankind is the highest commitment of which we are capable; it transcends the narrow allegiances of church, state, party,

3. Ibid.

4. Ibid., p. 17.

5. *The Humanist Manifestos I and II*, p. 18.

6. Ibid. p. 22.

class, or race in moving toward a wider vision of human potentiality.''[7] Such is the view of the humanist in the world today.

Let us pause here for a few moments to contrast this view of reality with that of God's revelation as recorded by Paul in his letter to the Galatians. Paul here contrasts two ways of looking at reality. One is the way of the flesh; the other is the way of the Spirit. One is the way of autonomous man, using his freedom as an occasion for immorality, impurity, sensuality, and disputing. The other is the way of the Spirit, the way of God, that issues forth in love, joy, peace, and self-regulation. The person in Christ, Paul says, has put the self-centered nature to death. His bondage to Christ brings freedom to live in a positive relationship with others. He has a humble estimation of himself (Galatians 5:26; 6:3). He realizes that his actions have eternal consequences (Galatians 6:8). He judges everything, not in relation to his own advantage, but in relation to the absolute standard of all truth, Jesus Christ (Galatians 6:2).

The methodology and conclusions of the naturalist send him down a dark road. He holds tenaciously to the value of man as man. But having killed God, his world view holds no reason for not killing man himself.

Naturalism can offer no valid reasons, given the nature of man, why he should be considered important. True, he is different from other things in nature, but he is essentially of the same material stuff as they. He has no divine spark. He is the product of time and chance, an unplanned biological accident. Having destroyed all basis for value, the naturalist in the end must view man as valueless also. The "God-is-dead movement" has become the "man-is-dead movement."

When philosophies presume to exalt man by centering themselves exclusively on man, they in the end debase,

7. Ibid. p. 23.

enslave, and exploit man. If there is no God to pass judgment on our actions, no Heaven or Hell, no objective truth and right except as we define them for our advantage, then we have warrant to unleash all the worst horrors of human nature. What presents itself as freedom from the restraints of God results in bondage to the self-interest of individual men.

As Richard L. Purtill has well put it,

> To reject the notion of a Person whose nature is the foundation of morality is ultimately to rob the notion of morality of any meaning. To do this is to give up any right to praise or blame, to call any action evil or any man good. And to do this is to become a troll rather than a man. Remove God from the universe and man does not step up to the empty throne, but instead steps down to the level of the beasts.[8]

8. Richard L. Purtill, *Reason to Believe* (William B. Eerdmans Publishing Company), p. 98.

# MORAL PESSIMISM

*Please read James 1:19-21; 3:13-18, 4:1-17, 5:1-3.*

The wresting of powers *from* Nature is also the surrendering of things *to* Nature. As long as this process stops short of the final stage we may well hold that the gain outweighs the loss. But as soon as we take the final step of reducing our own species to the level of mere Nature, the whole process is stultified, for this time the being who stood to gain and the being who has been crucified are one and the same.[1]

If you should be so bold as to dip into the offerings of your local library in the area of ethics, you would very likely be overpowered by the complexity and the variety of books that have been written on the subject. You might feel like a person who goes into a bookstore to buy a road map to help him drive his car to Chicago and is sold books

1. Reprinted with permission of Macmillan Publishing Co., Inc. from *The Abolition of Man* by C. S. Lewis. Copyright 1944, 1947 by Macmillan Publishing Co., Inc., renewed 1972, 1975 by Alfred Cecil Harwood and Arthur Owen Barfield.

on the history of Chicago, manuals for working on the internal combustion engine, books on the history of transportation from the Stone Age to the present, textbooks on petroleum engineering, books on the topography of Illinois, and books on the relation of the highway system to the economic outlook of the United States.

Much of the ethical literature seems more interested in the history of ethical philosophy, in isolating the ultimate base of ethical decision-making, and in defining the ultimate good than in giving useful help on how to live the good moral life. The Bible, by contrast, does both. It deals directly with the divine base of all ethical decision-making, and it gives clear directions as to how to behave in ordinary life, in relation to the divine base. We shall say more of this later. Let us take a look now at a few more of the philosophical paths that have created the confusion represented in the maze of today's morality.

## Nihilism

The naturalist, as we have said, saw man as made of the same substance as all physical matter and therefore without destiny. But he still held out for man's value on the basis of man's uniqueness, his self-determination, and his self-consciousness. These very things that set him apart as valuable, in the thinking of the naturalists, alienated him from his universe in the minds of the nihilists. If death means extinction, then life is without purpose and existence is absurd. Man is not valuable at all. Since man is nothing but matter, his vaunted knowledge itself is not to be trusted. The universe is totally impersonal and totally unaffected by man's actions.

Though people may act and think as if they were free, they are actually controlled by chance combinations of environment and heredity. Such is the opinion of the nihilist. Man is purely a cosmic accident, not knowing where he has come from or where he is going—but delighted to talk about it all the way, as if he really counted.

His importance is only an illusion. As James W. Sire puts it, to the nihilists "man is a conscious machine without the ability to effect his own destiny or do anything significant; therefore, man (as a valuable being) is dead."[2] Nothing remains of knowledge, ethics, beauty—or reality, for that matter. With the loss of meaning and value, there comes the loss of hope. Man is continually acting as if something important were happening or about to happen, but this is only an illusion. This theme became the basis for much of the drama in Europe following World War II.

The absurdity of the nihilist's world view is readily evident in the fact that he cannot even trust his prime assumption: "There is no meaning in the universe." If it is true, it is false. The nihilists find themselves with no frame of reference for reality. Soon they are not even sure of their own existence. As a drug user begins to have trouble distinguishing between material reality and his drug-induced world, the nihilist finds himself unable to distinguish the bounds of reality, dream, and fantasy. Taken to its logical (or illogical) end, nihilism is the stuff of mental illness. When one cannot distinguish objective reality from subjective reality he is in severe mental trouble. Not that all nihilists become lunatics. That would require more consistency than most are willing to exert.

## Existentialism

Into this pessimistic mental climate came the atheistic existentialist, seeking some way to bail man out from utter hopelessness. His answer is to divide reality into two sections: the objective, material world, and the subjective, inner world. Each world has its own logic, but it is the inner, subjective world that is the most important. Man first exists, then, during the course of his decision-making process, he adds definition to himself. The good,

2. James W. Sire, *The Universe Next Door* (InterVarsity Press, 1976), p. 81.

in the subjective sphere, is the consciously chosen action. It is completely subjective in that it is to be judged by no standard outside of the chooser himself. The problem with this is that it easily slips into the bewildering position that nothing really exists apart from what is in each person's head.

Since good is the action passionately chosen, Hitler, it seems, was good in his killing of the Jews. Existentialism assumes that the good will always be chosen, then circles on itself by defining the good as that which is chosen. Evil, in existential terms, is passivity—not seizing the initiative in one's life, letting others choose for us. Thus, logically, allowing God to choose good and evil for us through revelation would be the ultimate evil.

Theistic existentialism has had a profound effect on contemporary theology as well. It also divides experience into subjective and objective realms and emphasizes the subjective. Unlike atheistic existentialism, the subjective choice of faith is the important, self-authenticating choice. To the theistic existentialist, objective Bible history is not important. It could have happened or not. To him it really doesn't make any difference. The important things are not the historical facts but the timeless truths and fine examples of the Bible. The Bible is presented as pious mythology, untrustworthy as history but conveying truths of subjective importance.

### Emotivism

It may be well to stop here to mention another direction that God-denying subjectivism in moral philosophy has taken. This moral pathway, in its examination of man's moral nature, has concentrated on his moral language. The theory goes that when we say a thing is bad we are merely saying that we do not like it. Thus our moral statements are nothing more than statements of personal preference which bear no correspondence to any external reality.

My moral statements, in this view, are merely expressions of approval or disapproval. Among other things, they may be exclamations (expressing my unqualified approval), commands (expressing what I think you ought to do) or commendations (expressing my personal preference). The one thing they are not, however, is a reflection of some external reality. There is no way to argue whether my good is better than your good. Since each is subjective, each is equally valid and equally true. Like the existentialist, the emotivist ends with so many definitions of good that there is, in fact, none.

It is true, of course, that ethical statements do express feeling, evince attitudes, exert influence, issue prescriptions, guide choices, commend, recommend, condemn, and disparage—as the emotivists observe. The thing in dispute, however, is their belief that that is all they do. Those who would reject emotive theory as being inadequate would point out that in addition to the above, ethical language is also the language of comparison, comparison with some pre-determined ideal. When we use ethical language we are putting the action or object of which we speak within a category of actions which have something in common called goodness. If the action or object does not deserve to be in that category, we are not likely to be found commending it.

## Eastern Pantheism

It is an easy step from the view that ethical language is contentless to the ashrams of the East. "Perhaps," some have reasoned, "the way out of these dilemmas is to concentrate on being, not thinking. Maybe the problem is that man is always trying to approach the world with logic. Since reason, as the existentialists insist, cannot be trusted at all, why not stop thinking altogether?"

Westerners delight in their scientific method, in their technology, in their materialistic progress, and in the logical process of delineating and defining. The Eastern guru, however, seeks a path beyond definition and distinction. By his techniques he hopes to enter a new reality, oneness with the cosmos. Through contentless meditation, he wishes to pass beyond personality.

> The higher state is the state most approaching total oblivion, for one goes from the activity of ordinary life in the external world to the activity of dreaming to the non-activity, the non-consciousness, of deep sleep and ends in a condition which in its designation sounds like the reversal of the first three— 'pure consciousness.'[3]

Eastern thought shuns the categories of good and bad. Everything is; therefore everything is good and nothing is good. History has no meaning. Time is an illusion. Death is impersonal. Everything of value is eternal.

It is ironic that many young people have gone to the East looking for meaning and fulfillment in their lives. Yet these are contentless categories to the Eastern mind. The great goal of the East is nothingness, not fulfillment.

## Higher Consciousness

Along with the emphasis on the subjectivity of the East has come the search for a higher consciousness on more Western terms. The world, in this view, is irrational. Conventional knowledge is limited. Drugs and mystic techniques are used to bring about a mystical experience transcending time and space. Man's consciousness is the true center of the universe, and it has the ability to manipulate physical reality. Courses and experiments in parapsychology in leading universities give evidence to the popularity of this spreading philosophy.

Imagination is true reality. Altered consciousness— through drugs, music, meditation, and other tech-

3. Sire, *The Universe Next Door,* p. 139.

niques—offers entrance into an invisible universe transcending that known to the uninitiated. The mind and the imagination are the true keys to existence. "I believe; therefore it is." Believing is being. The self is absolute king and as king can do no wrong. Self-satisfaction is the only thing.

## Occultism

Into this stream also come the followers of the occult. Demons and devils, whether seen in psychological terms by the occultist as an extension of inner consciousness or in real terms as assistants in the control of the visible universe, become the ultimate reality.

It may, at first, seem strange that in this world of scientific knowledge and advancement the apparently superstitious should become so widespread. C. S. Lewis suggests a reason:

> There was very little magic in the Middle Ages: the sixteenth and seventeenth centuries are the high noon of magic. The serious magical endeavor and the serious scientific endeavor are twins: one was sickly and died, the other strong and throve. But they were twins. They were born of the same impulse. . . . There is something which unites magic and applied science while separating both from the 'wisdom' of earlier ages. For the wise men of old the cardinal problem had been how to conform the soul to reality, and the solution had been knowledge, self-discipline, and virtue. For magic and applied science alike the problem is how to subdue reality to the wishes of men: the solution is technique. . . . The true object is to extend Man's power to the performance of all things possible."[4]

4. Lewis, *The Abolition of Man*, p. 38.

The modern descendants of the alchemists, with their astrology, spells, fortune-telling, and demon worship are continuing examples of man's open rebellion against God. They show his desire, with the assistance of the forces of evil, to take control. The devil's bargain, however, as Lewis points out, calls for us to give up our souls for the gaining of power. But when we have given up ourselves, the power we receive does not belong to us. We have become the slaves of that to which we have given our souls.

## Folly

We have passed through interlocking chambers of horror: the predictable alienation, despair, aimlessness, and self-deception of those who seek to construct a morality without God. Without God there is no key to the universe, no key to meaning, no key to value. Without acknowledgement of an external standard of true time, we are left to wander aimlessly from clockmaker to clockmaker hoping that we can find one that knows the riddle of the fourth dimension. Each clockmaker presents the best work of his mind and hands for our observation. But without any outside standard we can never know whether to prefer one man's work over that of another. Even if there is a measure of uniformity among all the clocks, the possibility remains that all may be wrong. We have only the enthusiastic assertions of each clockmaker that he alone has unraveled the key to time. We are told that we must take his word for it. Why? We are never told.

Needless to say, there is much that is tragic about this new-age man, shouting his freedom from Judeo-Christian ethics while sinking into the mire of disillusionment, alienation, drugs, superstition, and pantheism.

Romans 1:21-32 traces the horrific results of the wisdom of men apart from God. When man serves the creature more than the Creator he cannot escape the corruptions of homosexuality, fornication, wickedness, covetousness, maliciousness, envy, murder, slander, juvenile delinquency, dishonesty, brutality, and loveless-ness. We find ourselves in an age when these things are as normal as the daily paper and the evening news. We live in a day when man-centered morality is not only indulged in but is pushed into homes, in the name of entertainment.

James saw the folly of wisdom that is apart from God. It is, he said, "earthly, natural, demonic" (James 3:15). The wisdom of this sort thrives on jealousy and selfish-ness and resorts to disorder of mind and spirit. The wis-dom that comes from God, to the contrary, issues in peacefulness, gentleness, right reason, honesty, mercy, and resoluteness.

Apart from relationship with God, man has no way to achieve the fullness of life for which his spirit longs. He is like a drowning man that cannot quench his thirst. Happi-ness and satisfaction always elude him. Selfish to the end, he seeks to get what he wants by violence and force.

Since he does not acknowledge God, he can never re-ceive the benefits that are promised the righteous through prayer. In his arrogance and self-centeredness, man re-ceives not the blessing of God but His opposition. He resists God and runs with the devil. There is no sorrow for sin and no repentance, because to do these things would be to acknowledge God and His authority. He de-spises the Lawgiver and the law and seeks on every occa-sion to discredit belief in God. He relies on himself and his powers, not knowing that life itself is his only by the mercy of God.

In truth it is only the Lord's will that really matters. Man's own life, for all his posturing of intelligence and wisdom, is not in his hands. His arrogance in himself and his boasting of his freedom ring hollowly out into the cosmos. Though he denies human responsibility and any way of knowing right from wrong, his own nature con-tradicts him. He knows, in his inner self, that his rebellion is wrong and empty. He will stand before the Judge of all, stripped naked of his arrogance and exposed in his sin. He knowingly chooses the wrong and develops a world view to justify his wickedness. But he does not impress God. The things he puts his trust in will vanish.

Is there no hope for such a man? Not while he remains in his wicked rebellion against God. His only hope is in receiving, in humility, the Word of God. It is the only thing that can save him. That Word must come into the very essence of his life, to remold him from within. It must be received and planted into his consciousness to replace the filthiness and wickedness that are the assured partners of disobedience and rebellion against God.

# MORAL PREOCCUPATIONS

**6**

*Please read Matthew 5:16-48; 6:19-21; 25:34-36, 40*
*Mark 7:20-22; Luke 6:27-38; 10:25-37; 21:34-36*

The essence of biblical morality is not a legal system, a written code, an abstract moral philosophy, but a spirit and a loyalty, a vision and faith, incarnate in the inexhaustible rich and varied personality of Jesus. It is this fact which has lent astonishing flexibility to Christian ethics, while ensuring that each new extension and application is kept true by being referred, at all points, to the mind and example of the Master.[1]

In the previous chapters we have looked at several approaches to ethics—approaches of those who believe that there are no external standards for judging right and wrong. In this chatper we will consider some of the characteristics of theories held by those who *do* profess belief in external, normative ethical principles. Of course such belief is held by Christians who look on the Bible as their moral guide.

1. R.E.O. White, *Biblical Ethics* (John Knox Press, 1980), p. 11.

These theories can generally be identified by the relative importance attached to one of the three components of any human action:

1. The motive for the action
2. The action itself
3. The results of the action

We can look at the intent, the content, or the consequences of any action as the primary grounds for our discussion of its rightness.

## Three Elements

Focus on the middle element, the action itself, was once much more popular than it is today. There was a time when there was general agreement about what actions were right and what were wrong. This consensus, in the West, was drawn from our Judeo-Christian heritage. The moral judgments from this heritage were received with little question as the common ground from which all moral people acted. C. S. Lewis called this objective moral code the *Tao* and professed to find it in many different cultures and religious systems. Under eight headings he listed common principles shared by all:[2]

1. The Law of General Beneficence (rules against murder, oppression, cruelty, lying, dishonesty, hatred; and for kindness, generosity, love).
2. The Law of Special Beneficence (love of marriage partner, brothers and sisters and other kin, loyalty to nation).
3. Duties to Parents, Elders, Ancestors.
4. Duties to Children and Posterity.

2. Reprinted with permission of Macmillan Publishing Co., Inc. from *The Abolition of Man* by C. S. Lewis. Copyright 1944, 1947 by Macmillan Publishing Co., Inc., renewed 1972, 1975 by Alfred Cecil Harwood and Arthur Owen Barfield.

5. The Law of Justice (sexual justice; against infidelity, dishonesty, and partiality in judgment).

6. The Law of Good Faith and Veracity (against lying and falsehood).

7. The Law of Mercy (concern for the weak, the handicapped, widows, orphans, hungry).

8. The Law of Magnanimity (courage, self-sacrifice, honor).

Ethical theories that concern themselves with given principles and rules for human action are known by a number of names: *deontological* (from the Greek word *deon* meaning ought), *ateleological* (not dependent on outcome), *formal* (from Immanuel Kant, who focused on the form an action takes, his major principles being to judge an individual action by whether it could be universalized to become a standard for all human behavior), and *absolutist* (suggesting the unchanging character of law, irrespective of circumstances).

Ethical theories that focus on results, by contrast, are concerned primarily with consequences. They are often called *teleological* (from the Greek word *telos,* meaning purpose or goal). They also may be called *utilitarian* in that they stress the ultimate usefulness of the action.

Ethical theories that focus predominantly on motive are not so common. This may be because motive merges with consequence when we are talking of the intent in an action about to be taken. Motive also merges with the middle element, action, when something is undertaken out of a sense of duty to the fixed standards of law.

## Problems

There are problems with an ethic that focuses primarily on motives. One problem is expressed in the common saying, ''Sincerity is not enough.'' We may undertake an action with the best of motives, only to find that the actual outcome is disastrous.

The Aswan High Dam in Egypt was built with the intention of improving the productivity of the country by providing needed irrigation. It brought thousands of acres of land under cultivation. But the result of the dam has been to upset the ecological patterns of the whole region. Fishing at the Nile's mouth has been spoiled. Since the Nile waters no longer carry a heavy load of silt, they move faster and are undercutting river banks and bridges. Land that was formerly fertilized by the annual floods must now be fertilized artificially. Snail fever has spread throughout the populace of Egypt. Lake Nasser, behind the dam, is filling with silt at an alarming rate.

Probably the motives of the Americans who designed the project were good. So were the motives of the Russians who built it, and the Egyptians who wanted it. That it has brought many acres under cultivation is observable fact; but that it was a good thing to build the dam remains open to question.

It is very difficult when planning an action to know precisely what its outcome will be. We may be wrong in our thinking. A well-intentioned action may turn out badly despite our best intentions. On the other hand, as with the actions of Joseph's brothers, an action intended for evil may turn out for good (Genesis 50:20).

We might argue that so long as we are looking toward a good end, we are vindicated no matter what the result may be. But it can always be argued that had we done our homework better (as is our ethical duty), had we studied the issues more carefully, had we better anticipated possible difficulties in the reaching of our declared objectives, we would have stood a better chance of reaching our true goal. Even though we may wish to stand on good motives when our intentions fail, we may be open to the charge of carelessness, insufficient observation and investigation, or faulty reasoning.

Further, we seldom find ourselves with complete purity of motives. Even the best of actions can be done from faulty motives. We may give to the poor in order to exalt our self-importance (Matthew 6:2). We may feed the hungry out of a grudging sense of duty, not love (1 Corinthians 13:3).

We frequently display a self-serving tendency to claim good motives for actions that actually come from our basest desires. I may say I refuse to pay my taxes because money is being squandered by government on evil things. In actual fact, I may be niggardly, selfish, and dishonest.

A basic problem with an overemphasis on motive is rationalization (we deceive ourselves and others as to our real motives) and opportunism (we adapt our actions and judgments in such a way as to further our personal interests without regard to principles or consequences). Another pitfall may be sentimentalism, an over-concentration on feelings.

An ethic that focuses predominantly on actions may also develop problems. It can lead to the elevation of rules and law above human values. When it is overemphasized, concentration on the importance of rules becomes legalism. The Pharisees of Jesus' day were an excellent example of this failing. They developed an extremely detailed code of right and wrong behavior. They constructed a law code that contained 248 commandments and 365 prohibitions. Their traditions came to be valued above the spirit of the law. While attending to the detail of the tithe in the smallest items, they neglected the important matters—justice, mercy, faithfulness (Matthew 23:23). In their quest for legal perfection, they lost sight of human values.

Not only did they use their traditions to insulate the content of the law, they used them also to circumvent the spirt of the law (Matthew 23:16-22). They became hairsplitters *par excellence,* ever watchful for some offense against their interpretation of the meaning of the laws. At the same time they devised clever ways to stay within the letter of the law while violating its spirit. The Sabbath regulations were good examples of both tendencies. The Pharisees identified lifting as work; and work was prohibited on the Sabbath Day. So they argued at length whether or not a father could pick up his child on the Sabbath Day. Travel was work, so they decided that one could not walk over seven-eighths of a mile on the Sabbath Day without being guilty of work. Then, since it was frequently to their convenience to go farther than that, they interpreted the tradition to mean seven-eighths of a mile from their personal property. This allowed them to drop pieces of pottery along their route so that they would never be more than seven-eighths of a mile from their property.

An emphasis on results also has some built-in problems. Our knowledge is finite and frequently faulty. At the point when we must decide, the point when we must perform or refuse to perform the action in question, we have little way of knowing what the eventual outcome will actually be. Further, as with the Aswan High Dam, there may be a number of outcomes, some good and some bad. How are we to judge between them? Results, like motives, are very difficult to assess.

Also the question arises as to whether we should count short-term or long-term effects. If long-term effects, how long must we keep our judgmental options open before pronouncing our estimation of rightness?

Let us suppose that some missionaries fly a plane into a primitive tribal area and make contact with the natives. When their plane lands, the missionaries are immediately killed. On the basis of results, should we judge that their decision to go was wrong in the first place? But wait. The wives of the missionaries go in and share Christ with the natives, who repent of the murders and accept Christ in great numbers. What seemed to be a bad decision redounds to the proclamation of the gospel. So maybe the men made a good decision after all. But then neighboring tribes persecute the new Christians and thousands die in tribal warfare. Because of these deaths, jungle fields are not cultivated. There is a famine. Still more people die. Now it seems that economic and physical havoc is the result of the action of those brave flyers. "But," says the Christian, "that is incidental, because many who have died have now gone to Heaven. This could never have happened without the sacrifice of the flyers."

So the debate continues event after event, generation after generation, as multitudes of interrelated causes and effects are assessed. It is an endless progression with finality never in sight. Who knows but what a seemingly endless progression of ill outcomes may at long last yield one gigantic good? If right and wrong are to be judged by consequences in their entirety, how do we know when all the pertinent information is in? How do we know enough—accurately enough and fully enough—to make our judgment?

There is still another problem for those who would focus on the result of the action. On what basis are the results to be judged either good or bad? Though he shuns the absolutes of the rule-conscious deontologist, the result-conscious teleologist must appeal to some standard outside the situation as the basis for his final ethical judgment. He must bootleg in some deontological principle such as he has renounced. I will talk of this more in next chapter's discussion of situation ethics.

## Bible Balance

We pause here to note that the Bible emphasizes motives, actions, and consequences. The tenth Commandment emphasized the desires of the heart by prohibiting covetousness. Thus it called upon the people of Israel to examine the attitudes from which actions spring. Samuel was told that God looked on the heart, not on outward appearances (1 Samuel 16:7). The Sermon on the Mount began with a listing of beautiful attitudes that are at the heart of Christian behavior (Matthew 5:1-12). Also in that sermon Jesus focused on the motive of the heart in His distinctive teachings about anger and murder, and lust and adultery (Matthew 5:21-28). He further said, "That which proceeds out of the man, that is what defiles the man. For from within, out of the heart of men, proceed the evil thoughts and fornications, thefts, murders, adulteries, deeds of coveting and wickedness, as well as deceit, sensuality, envy, slander, pride, and foolishness. All these things proceed from within and defile the man" (Mark 7:20-23).

The Bible continually emphasizes the importance of keeping the commandments of God. The law, to Israel, was absolute and irrevocable. The essence of the covenant relationship for the people of Israel was respect for the laws of God. The psalmist cried out, "Make me walk in the path of Thy commandments, for I delight in it" (Psalm 119:35). Jesus said, "Do not think that I came to abolish the Law or the Prophets; I did not come to abolish, but to fulfill. For truly I say to you, until heaven and earth pass away, not the smallest letter or stroke shall pass away from the Law, until all is accomplished. . . . For I say to you, that unless your righteousness surpasses that of the scribes and Pharisees, you shall not enter the kingdom of heaven" (Matthew 5:17-20). Jesus kept the commandments of God (John 15:10-15) and He expected His disciples to obey His commandments (John 14:15). To Jesus the keeping of God's commandments was equated with love. The importance of right actions was emphasized again and again by Paul (Philippians 4:9; 2 Thessalonians 2:15; 3:14; 2 Timothy 1:13). John wrote, "For this is the love of God, that we keep His commandments; and His commandments are not burdensome" (1 John 5:3).

There is, in Biblical ethics, a profound consideration for effects. The effects of keeping the commands of God were always beneficial, the results of disobedience always disastrous. "You shall walk in all the way which the

Lord your God has commanded you, that you may live, and that it may be well with you, and that you may prolong your days in the land which you shall possess" (Deuteronomy 5:33). "But if you do not obey Me and do not carry out all these commandments, if, instead, you reject My statutes, and if your soul abhors My ordinances so as not to carry out all My commandments, and so break My covenant, I, in turn, will do this to you: I will appoint over you a sudden terror, consumption and fever that shall waste away the eyes and cause the soul to pine away; also, you shall sow your seed uselessly, for your enemies shall eat it up. . . . And I will also break down your pride of power; I will also make your sky like iron and your earth like bronze" (Leviticus 26:14-19). Israel's obedience would also be noted by her neighbors (Deuteronomy 4:6).

Christians are to be shining lights in a dark world (Matthew 5:16). They are to seek to do positive good (Matthew 7:12). Paul instructed Christians to be watchful of actions that might be interpreted in such a way as to cause others to stumble in the faith (Romans 14:19-21; 1 Corinthians 8:9-13). Paul constantly examined his actions in light of his goal to reach the unsaved with the message of Christ (1 Corinthians 9:22); he sought not his own good, but the good of others (1 Corinthians 10:24-33).

The Christian, finally, conducts his life with regard to the final outcome, an eternal inheritance prepared for him from the foundation of the world (Matthew 25:34). All actions are in light of eternity, and in light of the reward of the righteous and punishment of the unrighteous.

The Bible avoids the weaknesses of one-element normative ethics by its emphasis on the importance of motives, actions, and outcomes. It is a balanced ethic calling for careful thought and the examination of every action in light of our intentions, in light of the commandments of God, and in light of its effect on our lives and those of others, both now and for eternity.

## Pleasure

We cannot leave our consideration of result-centered (teleological) ethics without some comment about pleasure. While the ultimate good has been viewed by various moral philosophers as duty, knowledge and reason, justice, harmony, survival value, rectitude, choice, God's will, co-operation, good will, temperance, courage, self-actualization, love, upright will, and many other virtues, the most persistent quality looked for in the outcome of actions has been pleasure. To some, the ultimate principle has been "If it feels good, do it." For others it has been "the greatest happiness for the greatest number."

Pleasure ethics comes in several varieties. Some people look for immediate gratification of personal desires. Others look for more refined, more long-range good. Some have attempted to create an equation intended to maximize pleasure and minimize pain. Some see the location of pleasure primarily in the individual (egoism), while still others would locate it in society (utilitarianism).

That pleasure is of great human concern needs hardly to be questioned. It is estimated that in 1978 the American people spent $91,200,000,000 in the pursuit of pleasure, and this year the figure is probably even higher. Yet there is nothing so deceptive as the pleasure principle for human conduct. In one of its most crass forms the egoistic variety of hedonism is illustrated today in the *Playboy* philosophy. William S. Banowsky, writing of it, says,

What most offended Jesus' contemporaries, and what modern men find even harder to accept, is His insistence that to find life we must first lose it. "We reject any philosophy," writes Hugh Hefner, "which holds that a man must deny himself for others." The playboy cult holds that every man ought to love himself preeminently and pursue his own pleasure constantly. Nowhere is the clash between popular playboyism and the ethical realism of Jesus any sharper than over how the good life is to be achieved. Hugh Hefner tells us to get all we can, Jesus tells us to give all we can. Because the clash is total, there is no way to gloss over it. The popular philosophy teaches that to get life you must grab it; Jesus taught that to win we must surrender. The conflict is absolute and irrevocable.[3]

Those who have made pleasure their highest aim, whether for the individual or the group, have always struggled to define what pleasure really is. In particular, those who have made "the greatest happiness to the greatest number" their ethical goal have foundered in their attempts to define the good they seek. Is it pure quantity of pleasure? Or is it quality of pleasure? Or duration? Or immediacy? Or certainty? Or how unadulterated it is with any pain? Or how likely it is to lead to further pleasure? Are some pleasures to be sought more than others? If so, on what basis? How does a person choose among the conflicting pleasure drives within his nature? Should he follow base, short-term gratification or aesthetic, long-term happiness? Might not one person's pleasure be another person's pain?

How does one weigh something so subjective as pleasure with any accuracy, as must be done if it is to be the basis for comparison and judgment? The Bible answers these questions by rooting pleasure in relationship with God and man. Joy is in the Lord, peace and contentment in Christ Jesus: "Rejoice in the Lord always; again I will say, rejoice! Let your forbearing spirit be known to all men. The Lord is near. Be anxious for nothing, but in everything by prayer and supplication with thanksgiving let your requests be made known to God. And the peace of God, which surpasses all comprehension, shall guard

3. From *It's a Playboy World* by William S. Banowsky copyright © 1969 by Fleming H. Revell Company. Used by permission.

your hearts and your minds in Christ Jesus" (Philippians 4:4-7). As the Hebrew proverb put it, "He who gives attention to the word shall find good, and blessed is he who trusts in the Lord" (Proverbs 16:20). It was not unfettered freedom that meant happiness to the Hebrews. Rather it was obedience to the laws of God: "Where there is no vision, the people are unrestrained, but happy is he who keeps the law" (Proverbs 29:18).

In our rejection of the pleasure-centered life, we must not forget that the Bible speaks a good deal about pleasure in this present life. Sex, for instance, is a good gift of God to man and woman (Genesis 1:27, 28, 31; 2:24; 1 Corinthians 7:3-5; Proverbs 5:18, 19; Song of Solomon). The Christian daily enjoys all the blessings that God showers upon him (Matthew 6:25-34). The center of his joy is the worship and adoration of God (Psalm 16:11). The Christian knows that the pursuit of pleasure for pleasure's sake is bound to be futile. Pleasure is a by-product of putting God and others first in our lives (1 Peter 3:10-14; John 10:10).

## Materialism

In addition to pleasure, as we have noted, many other principles have been proposed as the highest value for mankind. Materialism suggests that comfort and wealth are the way to pleasure and that they present the highest goals of life. This idea holds strong sway in America. The paradox of riches, like the paradox of pleasure, is that more is promised than delivered. Roger Rosenblatt, writing in *Time* magazine about the wealthy, noted, "After the big house and the big garden and the big animals, parties and people, what do most of the world's big spenders announce? That they are bored. *Bored*."[4] Those whose every wish is satisfied become satiated and cynical.

4. *Time,* December 8, 1980, p. 89. Copyright 1980 Time Inc. All rights reserved. Reprinted by permission.

Communism presents a different sort of materialism. When Marx talked of materialism, he was not talking of the accumulation of money and possessions. Marx's materialism was built, much like other forms of naturalism, on the assumption that matter is the only reality and that everything, including thought, will, and feelings, can be explained in terms of matter.

Both forms of materialism are opposed to the Bible perspective on the material universe. Marxian materialism denies the realm of the spiritual and sees all in material, physical terms. The Bible, however, recognizes the reality of the unseen world. "Now faith is the assurance of things hoped for, the conviction of things not seen. For by it the men of old gained approval. By faith we understand that the worlds were prepared by the word of God, so that what is seen was not made out of things which are visible" (Hebrews 11:1-3). There are spiritual forces of good and evil at work (Ephesians 6:12).

The Bible is equally forceful in discounting the ultimate value of material wealth. Man's treasures are to be laid up in Heaven, not on earth (Matthew 6:19-21). Life does not consist in beautiful clothes (Matthew 6:28-30) or in conspicuous consumption (Matthew 6:31, 32), or in property owned (Luke 12:15-21). (It is interesting to note how much advertising in our slick magazines is given over to these very things.) Jesus said, "You cannot serve God and Mammon" (Matthew 6:24). Yet despite the Bible's clear warnings about the danger of riches, the success ethic, as defined in possessions, has virtually become the creed of our land and, unfortunate to say, of many of our churches. Some have even defined spirituality in terms of God's material reward of the faithful.

In the next chapter we will take up situation ethics, a contemporary ethical theory much in fashion. Its prime good is love. It will be seen that situationism makes love an excuse for disobeying God's commandments rather than an incentive for obeying them.

# MORAL
# PRIORITIES

*Please read 2 Timothy 2:19-26; 3:1-7, 16, 17*
*Titus 2:1-15; 3:1-7.*

There can be no quarrel with the new moralists that God intends that a man love his neighbor and seek the good of others. However, the new morality and biblical morality part when the problem is raised regarding the *content* of love. Whereas the new moralists think that love must be defined by human beings and tailored to meet each situation, biblical writers hold that love is served by keeping the commandments of God.[1]

### Beliefs and Actions

Do our actions dictate our convictions, or do our convictions dictate our actions? I have noted in my college ministry that students from Christian backgrounds may begin to adopt the non-Christian life-styles that are so common on campus. For a while they live in two worlds,

1. From *The Morality Gap* by Erwin Lutzer. Copyright 1972. Moody Press, Moody Bible Institute of Chicago. Used by permission.

being one thing when with non-Christians and another when with Christians. Then, gradually, they begin to adopt moral philosophies that will allow the sinful actions in which they are involved. It may well be true that our ethical world view is more a product of our base desires than it is the product of our intellect, whether we are philosophers or plumbers, salesmen or secretaries.

It works the other way as well. Beliefs do affect actions. We have seen belief in Christ bring radical change to the life-styles of many. If our actions do not agree with our beliefs, we may find alarm bells of conscience constantly ringing. Our solution to this may be to bring our actions into conformity with our beliefs, or to bring our beliefs into conformity with our actions. If we can do neither, we are likely to suffer the things that send countless people to physicians and psychiatrists.

Why is our society now so infatuated with situation ethics? Is it because this gives people a philosophical position by which they can do what they want to do, or are people doing what they want to do because they have bought into the thinking of situation ethics? I have a feeling it is the former. Situation ethics, as presented by Joseph Fletcher, provides the perfect philosophical base for a permissive society.

## Situation Ethics

Situation ethics, on the surface, seems to give some principle of direction for action when rules of ethical conduct are in conflict. It is not difficult to imagine such situations. We may find ourselves, for instance, trying to decide whether obedience to our government is more or less important than obedience to our personal consciences. We can think of occasions when one might have to lie in order to save a life, as was done by many who hid Jews in Germany during World War II. By its one-absolute ethic, situationism seems to offer some help in these problem cases.

Situationism is not complete relativism. There is *one* absolute norm of human conduct as presented by Joseph Fletcher in his books, *Situation Ethics* and *Moral Responsibility*. That norm is love. The most loving action is the one always to be chosen.

Fletcher attempts to construct a theory of morality that avoids the problems associated with rigid rules on the one hand and with a complete absence of rules on the other. His solution is the one extremely general ethic that treads this narrow path and can be applied in all cases—love.

Fletcher sees each ethical situation as unique. While moral maxims may be of some general help, they are not sure guidelines in the complexities of real decision-making. Situations are so different that it is impossible to determine beforehand what right conduct should be. Morality can be judged only in its particular context. No external, anticipatory rules can ever be of much use, thinks Fletcher.

Fletcher also undercuts rules by his emphasis on people. Personal values are supreme, not rules or principles. "Treat persons as ends, never as means," he says. "Things are to be used; people are to be loved."[2]

Fletcher describes his theory as "Christian situation ethics," and there is much to it that sounds familiar to Christian ears. The emphasis on love certainly has a Scriptural ring. The Bible also has a strong emphasis on the importance of persons. But the problem is that Fletcher so uses his principles as to undercut completely any loyalty to Biblical commandments. By its emphasis on love to the exclusion of all else, situationism reduces and distorts Biblical ethics beyond recognition.

Traditionally, Bible students have talked of the different demands of love and justice. Both hold high place in

2. From *Situation Ethics: The New Morality,* by Joseph Fletcher. Copyright © MCMLXVI W. L. Jenkins. Used by permission of The Westminster Press.

the Christian mind, but they are sometimes in conflict. We see this in the nature of God, whose justice demands condemnation of man and whose love prescribes mercy. The Christian sees the sacrificial death of Jesus as bridging the gap between love and justice. Since Fletcher, however, desires one supreme element, he subsumes justice to love. Justice, to Fletcher, is love distributed. While there is certainly a connection between love and justice, this blurring of distinctions contributes to some of Fletcher's dubious conclusions in the application of his love principle to human situations.

Fletcher concentrates on results, not on rules or motives. He asserts unabashedly that only the end justifies the means. He does, however, cloud the issue by appealing to motive when it suits him. As Erwin Lutzer wrote,

> On the one hand Fletcher insists that the intention of the agent makes an act moral; while on the other hand, he maintains that an act is not moral until it helps someone. However, the two views cannot be reconciled. If an act is moral because of good intentions, then the consequences must be regarded as irrelevant. . . . When pressed to choose between the two methods of evaluating a moral act, situationists prefer to remain ambiguous. Fletcher uses both meanings throughout his writings, giving the impression that everything is perfectly clear. There is, of course, an advantage to such double-talk; it gives the moralist an opportunity to keep shifting ground in an ethical debate.[3]

To Fletcher, nothing is good or bad of its very nature. What is important is whether the result helps or hurts persons. He sees not a love of duty as his mainspring of conduct, but a duty to love. His is not a selfish love, but a

3. Lutzer, *The Morality Gap*.

giving love that seeks the greatest good for the greatest number. If the result is loving, it matters not what means has been used to achieve it. Fletcher writes that "no act apart from its forseeable consequences has any ethical meaning whatsoever . . ."[4]

Fletcher uses many stories to illustrate and prove his position. His critics note that his examples are highly unusual. Seldom would they come into the experience of ordinary people. For an ethic built on extraordinary cases to pass itself off as a system to be applied in everyday life is highly suspect.

On the surface, as we noted, Fletcher's ethic seems almost Christian. He quotes frequently from Scripture to give added strength to his arguments. Certainly the emphasis on love echoes the sayings of Jesus. With its emphasis on persons, situation ethics seems to be standing for the right in the midst of our increasingly impersonal and materialistic society. By its emphasis on circumstances, situationism recognizes that many decisions (like lying to get a friend to a surprise party) are related to their context.

## Problems

There are, however, serious problems in Fletcher's love-norm approach to ethics. One is that his love is so general that it is virtually without content. What constitutes love, after all? Fletcher's ethic, by its emphasis on consequences, suffers the problems of all result-centered ethics. Who can know with any certainty before or as he acts what will be the immediate or ultimate consequences of his actions? Further, if we are to decide what a loving consequence actually is, we must still invoke some outside standard against which to judge it. When we are told to do the loving thing, we are told no more than if we had been told to do the good thing. What remains to be done,

4. Fletcher, *Situation Ethics: The New Morality*.

in both cases, is to define what acts are properly to be called loving—and good. Fletcher succeeds in delaying judgment until some results are known, but then he draws on external standards to justify the thinking that a loving action has been done. His theory, then, does not answer the real question. It works no better when he shifts attention to motives. An external standard for judgment is still needed.

Further, Fletcher assumes that the actor is invariably dispassionate in his decision-making. This seems seldom to be the case. We desire some things above others. Since Fletcher's love ethic is so subjective, it is extremely prone to self-deception. So long as love is undefined in any concrete terms (and Fletcher wants it defined only situationally), it can be used to justify any action.

We have spoken earlier of the fact that actions may have multiple consequences, some good and some bad. In order to be sure that we were doing the truly loving thing, we would have to have complete knowledge of all aspects of present and future circumstances. Such knowledge is beyond us as humans. Then, too, there is the matter of long-range and short-range effects. Some things, like the dentist's drill, are harsh in the short range but beneficial in the long range.

Though Fletcher regards general moral maxims as helpful to human conduct, his illustrations seem invariably to demonstrate the importance of going against the rules. If this is so, then it would seem that these maxims are deterrents to right action rather than encouragements to it. His good, loving act always seems to be defined as the act that broke the traditional moral rule. Breaking the rule, then, is defined as the loving act. Law, to Fletcher, is a burden to be transcended rather than a beneficial benchmark to be treasured. Yet experience tells us that rules are of tremendous service to human behavior.

Fletcher sets up, for illustration purposes, fixed situations. He then proceeds to draw his conclusions on the basis of those fixed facts. But in real-life situations there is always the possibility of an intrusion that will change the equation entirely. God, another person, an unanticipated event—any of these may intrude to change the factors under consideration. Fletcher tells the story of a woman who killed her baby in order to protect the lives of those in a wagon train who might have been given away to hostile Indians by the cries of the baby. The murder, then, is seen as a good act because many were saved by the sacrifice of the one. But who is to say that help might not have come in another form to bring deliverance? And wasn't there always a possibility that they might have been given away to the Indians despite her sacrifice? The result was beneficial to the many, it would seem; but we cannot know that they would not have escaped without the baby's death. And who is really to say that the lives of the many settlers were more important than the life of one baby? Without knowing what that baby might have become, in terms of good to many, we cannot be sure that his mother made the best decision. Suppose that child had lived, had escaped the Indians, and gone on to discover a cure for a terrible disease that afflicted thousands. Faced with those objections, Fletcher can appeal to the mother's motive. But to do so is to shift ground and to conclude that the outcome was unimportant, a conclusion against the stream of Fletcher's general argument. To make his case seem plausible to the reader, Fletcher constructs his imaginary situations carefully, then focuses on the details most suitable to his purpose of undercutting traditional rules of conduct.

And why, we might ask, ought we to accept Fletcher's choice of love as the only absolute? Other reasonable philosophers, as we have seen, have chosen other values as their highest good. If Fletcher enters into discussion in this regard, will he not have to use some outside standard, some justification other than love for his reason? If he does, he will have appealed to a higher good. If he does not, his love ethic is merely arbitrary, standing on nothing but his preference.

## Bible Love

The Bible does speak a great deal about unselfish, giving love; but it is never love at the expense of obedience to the commands of God (Romans 13:10). It is always love *expressed* in obedience to the commands of God. In the midst of the Ten Commandments, God declares that He shows lovingkindness "to those who love Me and keep My commandments" (Exodus 20:6). And Jesus said to His disciples, "If you keep My commandments, you will abide in My love; just as I have kept My Father's commandments, and abide in His love. . . . You are My friends, if you do what I command you" (John 15:10-14).

Situation ethics has been used by many to justify the breaking of God's absolute commandments, particularly in the area of sexual morality. The claim that love is somehow involved is used to justify all kinds of lust and immorality. Paul, however, had better advice for the young. He wrote to Timothy, "Now flee from youthful lusts, and pursue after righteousness, faith, love and peace, with those who call on the Lord from a pure heart" (2 Timothy 2:22). Purity of heart comes only as we live in loving obedience to the will of God as expressed in His Word. We are to pursue love, certainly, but not the self-love that so often is passed off as giving-love in our society. Love is never divorced from righteousness, right living, and relationship with God.

The ways of the devil are deceptive. He is quite willing that his distortions contain some truth, if that is what is necessary for us to swallow his poisonous lies. In the Garden of Eden, he said to Eve, "For God knows that in the day you eat from it (the forbidden tree) your eyes will be opened, and you will be like God, knowing good and evil" (Genesis 3:5). This, of course, was true (Genesis 3:22). Satan's lie was not in the fact; it was in the value.

He implied to Eve, and she believed, that it would be a good thing for her to become like God. God knows good and evil by relating them to himself. That which is good is of His nature; that which is bad is contrary to His nature. This is God's unique prerogative as Lord and Creator of all. But when man began to relate good and evil to himself, he was hopelessly in trouble.

The Bible teaches that God-like love often takes the course of confrontation and correction. It is not mere sentimentality or "do-your-thing" acceptance (2 Timothy 2:25). Sometimes a Christian must be like a surgeon who cuts out diseased flesh in order that living flesh may experience health. Those who seek freedom from God only find themselves ensnared by the devil. Their freedom from the restraints of God is captivity to the designs of Satan (2 Timothy 2:26).

The morality maze of today sounds very much like the days described in 2 Timothy 3:1-7. The list of woes sounds almost like a description of a typical university campus: self-love, money-love, success-love, arrogance, reveling, rebelliousness, lack of love, back-biting, undependability, conceit, pursuit of pleasure.

A few people, indeed, hold a residual faith and form of godliness, but even they may see the universe as a closed system in which God is not operative (2 Timothy 3:5). To them the Bible is little more than a collection of beneficial myths.

Prostitution, promiscuity, pornography—all of these flourish. A great deal of learning goes on, but because the divine source of all knowledge is denied, truth and wisdom are never found (1 Corinthians 3:18-20). Textbooks are out of date before they are in print. Man, in his own intellectual, independent arrogance is "always learning and never able to come to the knowledge of the truth" (2 Timothy 3:7).

There was a time when our universities were firmly based on belief in the Scriptures and were designed to impart truth derived from careful study of God's Word. It was thought that values were the most important part of an educated man's training. But today values are scarcely taught at all. Arthur G. Hansen, President of Purdue University, recently said, "I think value education is probably the one missing ingredient in education. While education can provide a student with very important tools and ways to make a living, if the student does not have a value structure, it is like a ship that is completely equipped with all the most recent technology but does not have a rudder. In short, where is the ship going? What's the direction going to be?"

Paul knew that the only rudder for a life worth living is the revelation of God. It alone provides the "true time of the realm," the absolute standard for all understanding of the right and the good. It alone is profitable "for teaching, for reproof, for correction, for training in righteousness" (2 Timothy 3:16).

Christian ethical standards are to permeate the whole of society. Old people are to show the goodness of God in their lives (Titus 2:1-5). Young people are to be sensible and exemplary in their actions. Slaves are to be obedient and honest. All of this touches society with an influence that brings honor to God (Titus 2:6-10). Happiness is not to be found in the indulgence of low, worldly desires, but in subjection to God. Life is to be lived in the expectation of Christ's return.

Such a Christian consensus brings order and peace to a nation. It creates an atmosphere where good prevails and the fruits of goodness are received by the whole of society (Titus 3:1, 2). The opposite of the Christian consensus, however, has become the accepted way of our land. Paul's words to Titus describe it well: disobedient, deceived, enslaved by lusts and pleasure, full of malice, envy, and hate (Titus 3:3).

The Christian is aware, as we will see in more detail in later chapters, that it is not really his good conduct that will save him. No matter how good his conduct is, he does not deserve God's favor. It is only through God's mercy and grace, expressed through the sacrifice of Jesus on the cross, that we may hope for eternal life (Titus 3:5-7).

# MORAL
# PATHWAYS

*Please read Ephesians 4:17—5:10, 15-21*

If no close relationship exists between the individual and God, any requirement to obey His will is an intolerable imposition, and the fact that the Creator has a sovereign right to impose His wishes makes matters worse, not better. It is only when the broken relationship is mended, when the unwilling slave becomes a friend (or, in Paul's terminology, a son) that God's moral law becomes a delight instead of an irritant.[1]

The thing that makes a maze a maze is the fact that all the pathways give the appearance of leading somewhere. Most, however, are attractive dead ends. We may follow such false paths for some time with the feeling that we are making good progress, but eventually they reveal to us their false nature. We have been tricked. We struggle to find our way again, but without reference points we become more and more lost. There seems no rhyme nor

1. David Field, *Free to Do Right* (InterVarsity Press, 1973), p. 35.

reason to the world we are struggling through. As we come to the convergence of two possible paths, we have no basis for choosing one over the other. The outcome is hidden from us. All is confusion, frustration, and bewilderment.

This seems an appropriate metaphor for the man-centered moralities we have studied. They promise freedom from our decision-making perplexity, but they only add to the confusion of our lives. Without God, they offer no fixed point of reference. Despite whatever cleverness, ingenuity, and imagination they represent, they are merely false leads dead-ending into inconsistency, illogic, and arbitrariness.

## The Maze and the Maze-Maker

Suppose, however, that you possess the blueprint of the maze-maker's original plan. Suppose the only route to the end of the maze is clearly sketched on the blueprint. Suppose that the hedges of the maze are so high that one cannot see over them. Suppose also that this maze has some terrible hazards built into it, that wrong paths mean not only frustration, but possible death. You offer the help of the blueprint to your friend as you both approach the entrance to the maze:

*Friend:* I have heard the blueprint spoken about often. But quite frankly I doubt both its authenticity and its accuracy. When I was in college everyone laughed at the blueprint theory of mazemanship. My teachers taught me to rely on my own judgment, not on some musty old collection of strange sayings and drawings. Besides, I don't believe the stories I hear about the dangers lurking in the maze. Maze-phobia is one of the ridiculous by-products of blueprint mentality.

*You:* The blueprint offers the only chance for survival. The right path to the ultimate goal of the maze is clearly marked on it.

*Friend:* Nonsense! There are many right paths. And there is no goal. The maze is all there is. Every rational person knows that. Didn't you ever take a course in Alternative Maze-Ways at college?

*You:* But why disregard the map of the maze-maker?

*Friend:* I don't believe in the maze-maker. Hedges have always been. Natural forces created this maze. It's just an example of nature's doing its thing. With lots of time, the hedges just lined themselves up, the paths emerged, and all the regularity came about.

*You:* But the orderliness, the perfect unity, the beauty, the intricacy, the sense of purpose—all of these point to a maze-maker. Hedges are not eternal. Time and chance bring thickets, not hedgerows.

*Friend:* Well, even if, for the sake of argument, I grant that a maze-maker planted the place, that doesn't prove that the blueprint came from him.

*You:* Look at the blueprint with me for a moment. Now look at that part of the maze over there. See how accurate the blueprint is in every detail. Have you read any of the people who have examined the evidence of the authenticity of the blueprint? They have examined the maze-maker's signature on the blueprint, studied its draftsmanship, and checked its history. They say that it is without doubt the work of the maze-maker.

*Friend:* Second or third rate scholars! Reputable mazemanship always rejects the maze-maker theory. That's the way you know it's reputable mazemanship.

*You:* There are other things in the maze-maker's memoirs besides the blueprint. In my experience those things have been accurate to reality every time I have put them to the test.

*Friend:* What is reality?

*You:* But what about the man whose story is in the last part of the book of the memoirs? He came back from the other end of the maze and authenticated the blueprint.

*Friend:* Oh, him! He was invented to sell more blueprints. My professors showed me that he is a hoax. It's because of him that so many of you are taken in by the blueprint.

*You:* But his memory is still present with us. All who know of him speak well of his character. Who could dream up such a man out of intent to deceive? Honest . . . truthful . . .

*Friend:* If he was so good, why did he have so many enemies? And why was he assassinated?

*You:* Some say it was because he claimed to be related to the maze-maker. I believe he was, and that's all the more reason to believe what he says about the blueprint. Others seem to think his death had something to do with his role as authenticator of the blueprint and with the plan of the maze-maker. At any rate, the assassination attempt was unsuccessful.

*Friend:* What I really don't accept of what this authenticator said is that there is only one way through the maze. I simply won't believe that. Logic tells me to be more open-minded than that. "Give every path a try and see where it leads" is my motto.

*You:* But that can be dangerous in the maze. If you get started in the wrong way you may never be able to get back on the right path. And remember that there may be hazards at each turn.

*Friend:* I'll manage those things when I come to them. If indeed hazards exist at all, I can take care of myself.

*You:* But there is no other guide to the maze that comes close to having the credentials of the blueprint. What have you to lose in giving it a try?

*Friend:* It is too limiting. I need to make my own choices. I must have my freedom.

*You:* Your freedom is the freedom to be eternally lost in the maze. Mine is to be freed from all the hazards of the maze and to finally emerge from it ready for what lies beyond.

Such, it seems to me, is the dialogue between the Christian and the autonomous man of our day. The Bible, we Christians say, is the blueprint. It bears the marks of authenticity in its very nature. It alone offers meaning to life and promise of safe passage to life's goals. Its truth has been attested to by countless people who have carefully examined the evidence. It is authenticated by the testimony, life, accomplishments, death, resurrection, and continuing presence of Jesus. If it is not true, then there is no means of truth available to us.

You and your friend enter the maze, but soon part company. You carefully consult the blueprint at every juncture. You stop, occasionally, to read some of the personal experiences of the authenticator. Progress is not always easy. Sometimes it seems as if you are going in the wrong direction. It just doesn't seem right to you. The path doesn't always conform to your expectations. The authenticator's words come to your mind. He urges those who would master the maze not to trust their own intuition, but to rely on the path marked on the blueprint.

Your path momentarily intersects with that of your friend. The friend cannot believe the care you take at each decision-point as you stop to consult the blueprint before going left or right.

*Friend:* I warned you the blueprint would stifle your humanity.

*You:* There are many wrong paths, but only one right path. While you assert your freedom at every decision-point, you find yourself forever entrapped in the maze. It will hold you tenaciously and not give you up. Your freedom, thus expressed, leads you to ever-increasing bewilderment and despair. What you call personal freedom is nothing more than entombment in the maze.

*Friend:* Nonsense! You always talk as if there is an exit toward which we are moving. There is no exit. It's a closed system. It's not where we're going so much as the fact that we are going. There is no meaning to the maze other than what we give it.

*You (reading from the Book of the Memoirs):* "There is a way which seems right to a man, but its end is the way of death" (Proverbs 14:12).

Metaphors are tricky, and this one has its weaknesses. I have included it here only to suggest the uniqueness and the absolute centrality of the Bible for those who would seek to live life successfully. I mean to suggest that the Bible alone offers the principles necessary for survival through the bewildering hedges of existence. I do not intend to suggest, as some do, that God has a blueprint for each individual life. I have counseled too many people who spend their lives playing hide and seek with God as if He were forever hiding His will from them. They are looking for the one job, the one residence, the one marriage partner that God has ordained for them. In every difficulty they look to the externals of their lives to see if they are off the one divine path. But the Bible concerns itself with the inner man, with moral character, goodness, godlikeness, faith, and personal relationship with God. This, it seems to me, is what the Bible blueprint is all about. What I am trying to get at in the metaphor of the maze is what C. S. Lewis was thinking of in a metaphor of his own:

In reality, moral rules are directions for running the human machine. Every moral rule is there to prevent a breakdown, or a strain, or a friction, in the running of that machine. That is why these rules at first seem to be constantly interfering with our natural inclinations. When you are being taught how to use any machine, the instructor keeps on saying, "No, don't do it like that," because, of course, there are all sorts of things that look all right and seem to you the natural way of treating the machine, but do not really work.[2]

## Arrogant Man

The Christian boldly asserts that the ancient book, the Bible, holds the secret of right and wrong in human conduct. To many of the twentieth century this assertion seems quaint. "Surely," we are told, "we have at last outgrown all that! We live now in the post-Christian era. God is dead. Haven't you Christians heard? The Bible may have been all right back in the Dark Ages, but now we are enlightened. We know that nothing exists but what we can analyze with our scientific instruments. The Bible has some primitive ideas. It seems to think that man is responsible for his actions. We know better. Psychology tells us we are what we are because of our experiences in the home. Biology tells us we are programmed by our genes. Sociology and psychology tell us we are programmed by our environment. Evolution proves that we have no special significance. The Bible itself is nothing but pious myths dreamed up by primitive people. We can dream up better ones ourselves. It is a human book, evolving like any other. We are on the brink of an evolutionary breakthrough. In our new knowledge of DNA we hold the tool to the liberation of man from the uncertainties of nature. With our drugs and with genetic control we can create the kind of man we design on our drawing boards. We can control man's environment and thus program into him whatever we please. There is no longer any place or need for God. He was all right while He lasted, but we have outgrown Him!"

The arrogance of these thoughts and the self-importance they represent echo the "boastful pride of

2. Reprinted with permission of Macmillan Publishing Co., Inc. from *Mere Christianity* by C. S. Lewis. Copyright 1943, 1945, 1952 by Macmillan Publishing Co., Inc. Copyrights renewed.

life'' of which John wrote (1 John 2:16). The Christian replies that while we certainly have advanced in many fields far beyond the technology of the ancients (though they did some things we still cannot do), we have made no advances in our ability to deal with the implications of our knowledge. The human element is the weakest link in our vaunted achievement. When we are dealing with questions of ethics and morality, we are dealing with things that basically have not changed through the centuries. Scientific advances may come and go, but humanity struggles again and again with the same moral problems. The problem of thievery is basically the same whether done by buccaneers with cutlasses or businessmen with computers. Levels of sophistication change, but ethical dilemmas remain the same.

The Christian asserts confidently to a skeptical world that the teachings of the Bible, particularly those of Jesus and the New Testament writers, can never become outdated or irrelevant, for they touch the basic relationships of all humanity: harmony with self, harmony with nature, harmony with others, and harmony with God. Despite the protestations of its detractors, the Bible remains the touchstone of ethical discussion. Even those who reject its authority find themselves forced to relate their innovations and ''improvements'' to it.

## Bible Ethics

We should note as we approach the Bible that it is not essentially an ethical textbook. It is much more than that. Ethics is dealt with in a dynamic context of interpersonal and human-divine relationships. The Bible is not a code book, a legal treatise, or a depository of exhaustive legal precedents. Bernard Ramm put it this way:

The right way to approach Holy Scripture as a guide for Christian ethics is not to see it as a total handbook or an exhaustive dictionary of Christian ethics. The Bible does contain examples of the right kinds of moral decisions, the standard God expects of us, the sort of policies or attitudes we are to have, and patterns or models for our ethical decisions. Holy Scriptures gives us clues to the kind of moral and ethical thinking which is pleasing to God. By following this procedure we gain not only the specifics which Scripture teaches, but we gain policies so that we can come to a Christian understanding of those ethical situations not treated in Scripture.[3]

The Bible makes little effort to isolate ethics from history or theology. Aside from the Old Testament's books of law, the Bible's teachings on the good, the right, and the desirable are random and comparatively unsystematic. Many of the Bible's ethical teachings emerge from historical situations and from personal examples of men and women caught in the act of decision-making. Other moral teachings come from prophetic pronouncement delivered in a historical setting. Other moral teachings must be derived painfully by the modern Bible student as he applies Biblical truth to situations where no precise Bible precedent exists.

Since the Bible approaches ethics and morality in a manner different from that of secular philosophical discussion, we find ourselves with a rather awesome task in trying to isolate and clarify major moral teachings. To discuss Biblical morality is to discuss nearly the whole of Biblical revelation, for it is impossible to discuss Biblical morality without some understanding of the Bible's teaching about the nature of God, the nature of man, the nature of evil, and the nature of salvation. Biblical ethics always

3. Bernard L. Ramm, *The Right, the Good, and the Happy,* © 1971, p. 36; used by permission of WORD BOOKS, PUBLISHER, Waco, Texas 76796.

arises from theology and it never stands apart from it. Its approach is not so much, "Do this because . . ." as it is "because of this, do. . . ."

While I will not attempt, within the narrow confines of this book, a complete systematization of Biblical ethics, I will attempt to list some of the things the Bible identifies as right or wrong and to call attention to the theological underpinnings of Bible morality.

# Section 2:
# *BIBLICAL IMPERATIVES*

"SIN AGAIN! WHY CAN'T HE BE MORE RELEVANT TO OUR DAY!

# MORAL
# PREMISES

*Please read 1 Peter 1:13—2:3; Ephesians 1:3-14.*

The moral standard is the character of God. We understand more about goodness as we learn more about Him. To know His will clearly we need the light of special revelation, but all men, by virtue of their creation, have His moral law "written on their hearts." If they try to argue its influence away, and follow a different code, they are automatically in the wrong. God's will is not one option among many.[1]

In the previous chapters we have seen the futility of any attempt to construct an ethic that leaves God out of its calculations. Man cannot explain his moral nature or define principles of value without some outside reference point. Satisfactory answers as to the nature of man and the purpose of man always lie outside the unaided wisdom of man. Thus the answers must come from outside, in the form of a message—or a messenger. The Christian

1. David Field, *Free to Do Right* (InterVarsity Press, 1973) p. 23.

believes that such a message from outside does, in fact, exist (in the form of the Bible) and that, in fact, such a messenger has come (in the form of Jesus Christ).

## Bible Revelation

The fundamental truth of Scripture is that God has revealed himself. God has chosen to make His mind known to us, to reveal His nature to us, to reveal His way of looking at things to us, to interact with us, and to reveal the nature of all reality to us. It is not our minds, our experiments, or our observations that can reveal what goodness truly is and why we should do good.

It is true that nature, by its variety, order, and complexity, points towards a Creator. It is also true that ethical sensitivity seems written into the heart of all mankind. But nature is essentially mute in matters of right and wrong; and human nature is essentially flawed in its ability to identify the right without self-deception and flawed in its ability to do the right that it knows.

The Bible, standing apart from all other literature, is the Word of God, the revelation of God. It is not dated or obsolete. As Isaiah noted, "The grass withers, the flower fades, but the word of our God stands forever" (Isaiah 40:8). The writer to the Hebrews spoke of Scripture's unique ability to cut to the heart of man's intentions and motives: "For the word of God is living and active and sharper than any two-edged sword, and piercing as far as the division of soul and spirit, of both joints and marrow, and able to judge the thoughts and intentions of the heart" (Hebrews 4:12). Further, Paul wrote to Timothy, "All Scripture is inspired by God and profitable for teaching, for reproof, for correction, for training in righteousness; that the man of God may be adequate, equipped for every good work" (2 Timothy 3:16, 17). Scriptural revelation, then, is the only adequate base for equipping ourselves to judge and do the right. It must systematically be fed into our minds, hearts, and consciences. Bible reading and Bible memorization are essential to the living of the good life. God's mind on things will do us little good if it remains only within the leather covers of a book. The Bible is designed to live within human skin, to be seen and read by unbelievers, as God's people bring to bear His mind, His will, and His purposes in the everyday decisions of their lives.

## The Foundation

Have you ever been around a child who discovers, for the first time, the word, "Why"? It can be an exasperating experience. The problem is that we give "what" answers to "why" questions. If someone should persist in asking "Why?" we would go on forever. For instance, a child standing beside a river asks, "Why is the river higher than yesterday?" You reply, "Because it rained last night." You expect the child to be satisfied with that, but he says, "Why did it rain last night?" You reply, "Warm air can hold more moisture than cold. The warm air near the ground rose, cooled, and lost its moisture in the form of rain." The child persists, "Why does warm air hold more moisture than cold air?"

So it can go on and on until you give up and disengage the conversation. The point is that each of your answers is a "what" answer that never fully satisfies a "why" question. It is an observation of what is happening, but it leaves unexplained why things exist as they do and why they have the observable properties they have. In normal conversation, by mutual consent, we break off our insistence on the why of things long before exasperation sets in. We finally accept a "what" answer as sufficient to satisfy the level of our curiosity. But science is built on the continual search for the next "why" with the understanding that still another lies beyond. The Christian is also engaged in this quest, though he does finally come to his ultimate answer, an answer rooted in the nature of God. The final answer must always be, "Because God made it that way, because God wanted it that way, because that is the way God is." Every theory of man's existence and nature stops asking "why" at some point. That point marks the basic presuppositions of that theory. The Christian pushes his quest for explanations to the existence and nature of God (Hebrews 11:6).

The foundation for all Biblical teaching on human conduct is the nature of God. Through Moses, God said to the people of Israel, "You shall be holy, for I the Lord your God am holy" (Leviticus 19:2). This was repeated by Peter in the New Testament when he wrote, "As obedient children, do not be conformed to the former lusts which were yours in your ignorance, but like the Holy One who called you, be holy yourselves also in all your behavior; because it is written, 'You shall be holy, for I am holy' " (1 Peter 1:14-16).

David Field put the truth in these plain terms:

> If we want to discover what goodness is all about, the Bible directs us not to some dusty old textbook on a library shelf, bulging with abstract ethical theories, but to the personal nature of the living God. Unlike any other moral teacher, God is utterly consistent. What He wills He is. Something is good not just because He commands it as part of His will, but because He exemplifies it as part of His nature.[2]

The goal of Biblical morality is, startlingly, nothing less than God-likeness. We receive His commands, not because they are basically useful or because they are productive of predictable social order (though they certainly are these things), but because these divine directives will enable us to bring our character into conformity with God's.

2. Field, *Free to Do Right*, pp. 15, 16.

It is clear from the Bible that God wants not so much a certain kind of conduct as a certain kind of person. The conduct is often easier to manage than the person. We can put on a front of good works and give lip service to high moral standards, but the process of allowing God to mold us into His likeness is much more challenging and frightening. God wants more than our conduct; He wants us!

The truth that moral conduct is grounded in the very nature of God leaps out from the teaching of Jesus. "But love your enemies," He says, "and do good, and lend, expecting nothing in return; and your reward will be great, and you will be sons of the Most High; for He Himself is kind to ungrateful and evil men. Be merciful, just as your Father is merciful" (Luke 6:35, 36). God sends His sun and rain on the unrighteous as well as the righteous. Therefore we are to love and pray for our enemies (Matthew 5:44-47).

Why are we to be generous? Because God is generous. Why are we to be forgiving? Because God is forgiving. Why are we to respect human life? Because human life reflects God's nature. Why are we to do loving things? Because God is love. Why are we to tell the truth? Because God is truth. Why are we to plan for regular rest? Because God, following creation, rested. Why are we to watch our words for truth, respect, and kindness? Because that is the way God communicates with us.

David Field wrote, "Many moralists urge, 'Do what I tell you.' A few would dare to say, 'Do as I do.' But God goes further. He says, 'Be as I am.' "[3]

In the New Testament, Christians are frequently called children of God or sons of God (Matthew 5:9; Luke 20:36; John 1:12; Romans 8:14, 16, 21; 9:26; Galatians 4:7; Philippians 2:15; 1 John 3:1, 10). These terms suggest that Christians partake of the nature of God, that they bear a

---

3. Field, *Free to Do Right,* pp. 16, 17.

family resemblance to Him, and that they are in close relationship with Him. The term "son of" was used by the Hebrews in a special descriptive way much as we use adjectives in English. For example, Mark 3:17 records that Jesus called two of His disciples "Sons of Thunder," probably because as young men they were loud and aggressive. Likewise in Acts 4:36 Barnabas is called "Son of Encouragement" because of his magnanimous, sympathetic character. So, in a sense, when we become "sons of God" we are becoming godlike.

In one of the most striking and startling statements in the New Testament, Jesus said, "Therefore you are to be perfect, as your heavenly Father is perfect" (Matthew 5:48). That nearly takes our breath away. We are human after all. Jesus was the only human being ever to live a perfect life. How can He expect that of us?

The Greek word for *perfect* in this verse has nothing to do with abstract, philosophical perfection. It is the perfection of design or function. The word is used to describe a mature student, a full-grown man, or an animal without blemish. It suggests that something is admirably fulfilling the task for which it was designed. We bumped into the word earlier when we were looking at ethical theories that concentrate on outcome or result. The noun is *telos* and the adjective *teleios*. As we noted then, the word has the idea of purpose, goal, end, or aim. For us to be perfect in the sense of *teleios* is for us to fulfill the purpose for which God designed us. God created us in His likeness (Genesis 1:26, 27) and only in becoming like God, within our human limitations, can we realize our full potential. William Barclay wrote:

> It is the whole teaching of the Bible that we only realize our manhood by becoming godlike. The one thing which makes us like God is the love which never ceases to care for men, no matter what men do to it. We realize our manhood, we enter upon

Christian perfection, when we learn to forgive as God forgives, and to love as God loves."[4]

At the risk of belaboring this point, let us be very clear in our understanding. God did not give us commandments, naming some things as good and others as bad, according to arbitrary whim. He gave us revelation as to right and wrong so that we can identify things as they truly are in relation to Him. God is the standard by which all things are to be judged. His nature is the nature to which we aspire. His thoughts are the standard of all good thought. That which is contrary to His way of looking at things is, by definition, wrong. Those things that are in harmony with His nature bring good results; those that are out of harmony with Him bring destructive results.

Frequently we look at Biblical commands as necessary impingements on our freedom. But they are designed not to bring us to bondage but to free us from it. God's commands keep us from being deceived by the immediate, the superficial, the short-lived, the false, and the enslaving. His commands keep us from actions that appear on the surface to be beneficial to us, but that are in reality designed for our destruction. Disobedience to God, while promising freedom, brings bondage to sin and death. Our modern society, in its insatiable desire for the freedom to do whatever it wants, finds itself in bondage to disillusionment, fear, hopelessness, sin, and death.

4. From *THE GOSPEL OF MATTHEW*, Volume 1, Translated with an Introduction and Interpretation by William Barclay. First published by The Saint Andrew Press. Published in the U.S.A. by The Westminster Press. Used by permission.

# MORAL PRINCIPLES

*Please read Romans 12:1-5, 9-21; 13:1-14.*

> God does not require a perfect, sinless life to have
> fellowship with Him, but He does require that we
> be serious about holiness, that we grieve over sin in
> our lives instead of justifying it, and that we ear-
> nestly pursue holiness, as a way of life.[1]

The Bible has its own special terminology and its own
special way of looking at human conduct. To many in
today's world, that terminology is archaic and "unscien-
tific." Terms like sin, salvation, holiness, sanctification,
righteousness, justification, and reconciliation speak of
spiritual realities generally ignored by the modern mind.

Even some faithful church members may tend to yawn
and go into intellectual hibernation at the mention of another sermon or study on righteousness, self-control, and
the judgment to come (Acts 24:25). Often it is difficult for
us to catch the life-and-death significance of the Bible's
teaching about these things. It is hard for us who have

1. Jerry Bridges, *The Pursuit of Holiness* (NavPress 1978), pp. 40, 41.

heard these terms often to recognize how world-changing these concepts were to the ancient mind and to understand how pivotal they are to our understanding of man's true nature and destiny.

The prophet Micah wrote, "He has told you, O man, what is good; and what does the Lord require of you but to do justice, to love kindness, and to walk humbly with your God?" (Micah 6:8). Micah clearly understood that God in His sacred Word, the Scriptures, tells man concerning the good. God has not left man to grope unaided for moral insight (Hebrews 4:12; 1 Thessalonians 2:13; 2 Timothy 3:16, 17). This underlines for our thinking the fact that God takes a personal, direct interest in our behavior, that He wishes us to have judicial information that He alone can supply, and that He has specific requirements for our daily conduct. God exists and is neither silent nor uninterested (Hebrews 11:6).

## The Walk, the Way, the Will

To Micah, one element of moral behavior was walking humbly with God. This is an often-recurring expression for conformity to the way and the will of God. It suggests identification with God, unity with God, partnership with God, and kinship with God. The psalmist heard God saying, "Oh that My people would listen to Me, that Israel would walk in My ways!" (Psalm 81:13). And in the joy of his spirit, the psalmist cried out, "How blessed are those whose way is blameless, who walk in the law of the Lord. How blessed are those who observe His testimonies, who seek Him with all their heart. They also do no unrighteousness; they walk in His ways" (Psalm 119:1-3).

Moses, after reading the Ten Commandments to the people of Israel, said, "So you shall observe to do just as the Lord your God has commanded you; you shall not turn aside to the right or to the left. You shall walk in all the way which the Lord your God has commanded you, that you may live, and that it may be well with you, and that you may prolong your days in the land which you shall possess" (Deuteronomy 5:32, 33).

David's last words to his son, Solomon, emphasized the same thing: "And keep the charge of the Lord your God, to walk in His ways, to keep His statutes, His commandments, His ordinances, and His testimonies, according to what is written in the law of Moses, that you may succeed in all that you do and wherever you turn" (1 Kings 2:3).

This was likewise the recurring theme of the prophets. Through Jeremiah the Lord said, "But this is what I commanded them, saying, 'Obey My voice, and I will be your God, and you will be My people; and you will walk in all the way which I command you, that it may be well with you' " (Jeremiah 7:23). Through Ezekiel God said, "I am the Lord your God; walk in My statutes, and keep My ordinances, and observe them" (Ezekiel 20:19).

The New Testament also describes behavior pleasing to God as a walk. Jesus said, "I am the light of the world; he who follows Me shall not walk in the darkness, but shall have the light of life" (John 8:12). Paul saw baptism as a burial with Christ that brings one to "walk in newness of life" (Romans 6:4). As one crucifies the flesh with its passions and desires, he begins to "walk by the Spirit" (Galatians 5:25). Paul saw Christians as God's "workmanship, created in Christ Jesus for good works, which God prepared beforehand, that we should walk in them" (Ephesians 2:10). He further urged the Ephesians, "Therefore be careful how you walk, not as unwise men, but as wise, making the most of your time, because the days are evil. So then do not be foolish, but understand what the will of the Lord is" (Ephesians 5:15-17).

To walk in the ways of God is to do God's will. Jesus was our example in seeking to conform His life to the will of God (John 5:30; 6:38). He instructed His disciples to pray that God's will might be done on earth (Matthew 6:10). He taught that not all who make show of religion will enter into God's kingdom, but only those who do the will of the Heavenly Father (Matthew 7:21). "Prove yourselves doers of the word" (James 1:22).

Paul contrasted foolishness with an understanding of the will of God (Ephesians 5:17). He prayed that Christians might be "filled with the knowledge of His will in all spiritual wisdom and understanding," so that they might walk in a manner worthy of the Lord (Colossians 1:9, 10). Christians are to do the will of God from their hearts (Ephesians 6:6); and their transformed natures make it possible for them to know that which is good, acceptable, and perfect (Romans 12:2). The person who does the will of God abides forever (1 John 2:17).

It is the clear claim of Scripture that a standard for human behavior exists outside of man himself. That standard is the revealed will of God. The touchstone for all ethical decision-making is God, His nature, His way, His will. Any ethic that refuses to take God into account is doomed to failure. Any ethic that distorts His teaching is unsound. Theology and ethics are intertwined in the Bible. God is not some abstract first principle, not some archaic myth, not some outdated superstition. He is Lord of the universe, living, active, concerned, involved in His creation. Everything that is done is under His scrutiny (Hebrews 4:13). What is done, whether in accordance with His will or in violation of it, has eternal consequence. One of the most heartening and at the same time the most frightening truths about God is that He is vitally concerned about man.

## Sin and Its Kin

To stray from the way of God, to violate the will of God, to act in a manner contrary to His nature—these are described in Scripture as sin. Basically, *sin* means failure. In classical Greek it meant to "miss the mark" as when a spear misses its target. Paul used the term at least sixty times to describe conduct that displeases God.

In the New Testament, *sin* describes a state of existence from which sinful actions come. In our sinful state we are all under sin's power, as a slave is under the control of his master (Romans 6:6, 14, 17, 20), as subjects are dominated by their king (Romans 5:21), or as a prisoner of war is at the mercy of his captor (Romans 7:23). Apart from Jesus, we are in the grip, under the power, under the domination, under the sway of sin.

Sin is connected in Scripture with blasphemy, insult of God (Matthew 12:31). It is linked with deceit (Hebrews 3:13; James 1:14-16), and desire for those things that should not be desired (James 1:14, 15). It is rebellion against God, lawlessness (1 John 3:4).

Sin has a deadening effect on man. It can lead to a "hardening of the heart," a sclerosis of the sensibilities (Hebrews 3:13). The final result of sin is death (Romans 5:12; 6:16, 23; James 1:15).

*Evil* is another Bible word for conduct that is displeasing to God. Evil is that which is bad. It can mean things that cause distress and discomfort, but it can also refer to moral badness. God's word to Judah by the mouth of Isaiah was, "Wash yourselves, make yourselves clean; remove the evil of your deeds from My sight. Cease to do evil, learn to do good; seek justice, reprove the ruthless; defend the orphan, plead for the widow" (Isaiah 1:16, 17). Those who do evil are storing up for themselves the wrath of God for the Judgment Day (Romans 2:5-10). We need to be on guard, lest we do evil when we want to do good (Romans 7:19).

The Christian is urged to overcome evil with good (Romans 12:21). Paul desired that the Romans be "wise in what is good, and innocent in what is evil" (Romans 16:19). The secret of the good life is to turn away from evil and to do good, "for the eyes of the Lord are upon the righteous, and His ears attend to their prayer, but the face of the Lord is against those who do evil" (1 Peter 3:10-12).

Another Biblical word for actions displeasing to God is *iniquity*. Eleven Hebrew words are translated by our English word *iniquity* in the Old Testament. The commonest Hebrew word has the idea of crookedness, perverseness, or going astray. The psalmist wrote, "Pardon my iniquity, for it is great" (Psalm 25:11). In the New Testament, the King James Version sometimes reads "iniquity" where the New American Standard more accurately translates "lawlessness" (Romans 6:17-19) or "unrighteousness" (1 Corinthians 13:6). Unrighteousness is identified as sin (1 John 5:17) and results in exclusion from the kingdom of God (1 Corinthians 6:9, 10).

Another common Bible word for evil is *wickedness,* our English translation for many Hebrew and Greek words. It was the wickedness of man that caused God to destroy Noah's world with the flood (Genesis 6:5). Wickedness is one of the evil things that Jesus identified as coming from the heart of the sinner (Mark 7:21, 22).

Paul made it clear that it is really the devil who is behind wickedness when he wrote, "Put on the full armor of God, that you may be able to stand firm against the schemes of the devil. For our struggle is not against flesh and blood, but against the rulers, against the powers, against the world-forces of this darkness, against the spiritual forces of wickedness in the heavenly places" (Ephesians 6:11, 12). As we seek to do the good, we are involved in a cosmic conflict in which Satan seeks to lead us into disobedience and rebellion against God. We cannot, however, escape responsibility for our actions by claiming that we are the helpless victims of Satan. We have individual responsibility (James 1:12-16) and are provided by God with the resources to resist Satan, if we will avail ourselves of them (1 Corinthians 10:13; 1 Peter 5:8, 9).

Space would fail us were we to attempt here to develop fully a study of Satan, sin, corruption, pollution, evil, iniquity, ungodliness, wickedness, unrighteousness, worldliness, the deeds of the flesh, and all the evils mentioned in Romans 1:18-32, Galatians 5:19-21, and other passages of Scripture. Suffice it to say here that the Bible clearly calls for good moral conduct. It is a major concern of God, and therefore it ought to be a major concern of man. In the next chapter we will try to look at some of the particular behaviors God clearly labels as right and wrong.

## Righteousness

Daniel said to Nebuchadnezzar, king of Babylon, "Therefore, O king, may my advice be pleasing to you: break away now from your sins by doing righteousness, and from your iniquities by showing mercy to the poor, in case there may be a prolonging of your prosperity" (Daniel 4:27). The concept of righteousness is one of the richest in the Bible. *Righteous* or *righteousness* occurs over five hundred times in the Old and New Testaments. The common Old Testament word translated *righteousness* partakes of the idea of justice. The common New Testament word translated *righteousness,* like our words *morality* and *ethics,* has as its root meaning "custom"; but that does not mean that what is customary is necessarily right. Righteousness is the will, intention, and desire to do the right. It implies justice (Psalm 72:2; 106:3; Proverbs 8:20) and integrity (Psalm 15:2). The psalmist wrote, "He loves righteousness and justice; the earth is full of the lovingkindness of the Lord" (Psalm 33:5). God guides His people in the paths of righteousness (Psalm 23:3). God himself is righteous, therefore He loves righteousness and hates wickedness (Psalm 11:7; 45:7). The person who pursues righteousness and loyalty will find life, righteousness, and honor (Proverbs 21:21). It is righteousness that exalts a nation (Proverbs 14:34).

Jesus urged His disciples to seek first God's kingdom and His righteousness (Matthew 6:33). The world is going to be judged in righteousness by Jesus (Acts 17:31). Paul wrote to the Romans, "Therefore do not let sin reign in your mortal body that you should obey its lusts, and do not go on presenting the members of your body to sin as instruments of unrighteousness; but present yourselves to God as those alive from the dead, and your members as instruments of righteousness to God" (Romans 6:12, 13). The kingdom of God is righteousness, peace, and joy in the Holy Spirit (Romans 14:17). Righteousness is to be diligently pursued (1 Timothy 6:11; 2 Timothy 2:22). The Bible is useful for training in righteousness and equipping for good works (2 Timothy 3:16, 17). Jesus' death has made it possible for us to live to righteousness (1 Peter 2:24). Ray Stedman wrote,

> Unfortunately, "righteousness" is one of those great biblical words which is little understood today. Most of us think of it as "doing what is right," and certainly that is part of its meaning. But the essence of the term goes much deeper. Its basic idea is "being what is right." One *does* what is right, because one *is* right—that is the biblical idea of righteousness. Righteousness is the quality of being acceptable to and accepted by God—fully and without reserve.[2]

## Holiness

While *righteousness* has overtones of justice, there is a companion term, *holiness*, that has overtones of purity and separation. In its various forms, it occurs over six hundred times in the Bible. The Christian puts on a new self in the likeness of God, created in righteousness and holiness (Ephesians 4:24). The term is frequently used in the Old Testament to call attention to God's uniqueness

---

2. Ray Stedman, *Authentic Christianity*, copyright © 1977, p. 70; used by permission of WORD BOOKS, PUBLISHER, Waco, Texas 76796.

(Isaiah 6:3). Moses sang, "Who is like Thee among the gods, O Lord? Who is like Thee, majestic in holiness, awesome in praises, working wonders?" (Exodus 15:11). Things and places set apart to this Holy God themselves become holy (Exodus 30:25; 35:19). God's holiness is the incentive and basis for human holiness (Leviticus 11:44; 19:2). God disciplines those whom He loves, that they may share in His holiness (Hebrews 12:10). Paul calls upon the Corinthians to cleanse themselves of all defilement of flesh and spirit and thus perfect holiness in fear of God (2 Corinthians 7:1). The Lord establishes the hearts of the faithful "unblamable in holiness" (1 Thessalonians 3:13).

Israel was a holy nation unto God, unique among all nations. Jesus brings all believers into the same sanctified relationship with God (1 Peter 2:9). The term *sanctification* applies to those who are holy, pure, and set aside to God's glory. They are saints. Peter identified Jesus as the "Holy and Righteous One" (Acts 3:14), and the writer of Hebrews saw Him as "a high priest, holy, innocent, undefiled, separated from sinners and exalted above the heavens" (Hebrews 7:26). The Christian is chosen and made holy by God (Colossians 3:12). The Holy Spirit takes up His abode in the hearts of believers and is contributing to the work of each believer.

## Sacrifice, Service, and Subjection

Paul wrote, "I urge you therefore, brethren, by the mercies of God, to present your bodies a living and holy sacrifice, acceptable to God, which is your spiritual service of worship" (Romans 12:1). He saw morality not so much as a list of do's and don't's as a relationship with a holy God. The Christian is to be different from other people.

He possesses a transformed mind that is regulated by the will of God. He therefore can discern what is good, acceptable, and perfect (Romans 12:2). There is to be a humility and unity about the fellowship of believers. Evil is to be abhorred; God is to be sought. Love is to be exercised. Generosity, hospitality, forgiveness, joy, perseverance, prayerfulness, empathy, concern, humility, peace, respect, goodness—these set the Christians apart from their society. Christians are to be loyal citizens, recognizing that government is an institution of God for the benefit of mankind (Romans 13:1-7). Love is the fulfillment of the law (Romans 13:8-10).

The Christian is to put on the Lord Jesus Christ (Romans 13:14). He is to take on Christ's nature and characteristics. He is to follow in Christ's steps. He is to view things as Christ viewed them. He is to bring his desires into conformity with the nature and teaching of Christ so that he is clothed in the very nature of Jesus. What results from this contact with Jesus is not a man who is a legal expert, but a man who is transformed into Christlikeness.

# MORAL PARTICULARS

*Please read Leviticus 19:1-6, 9-18, 32-37;*
*1 John 1:6—2:16.*

The main principles of the Book of the Covenant
are thus philanthropy and equity, reinforced by
piety, a fair summary of the whole trend of Old
Testament ethics.[1]

In the last chapter we sketched Biblical ethics in very
broad outline, considering some Bible terms and concepts
relating to human behavior. It is our purpose in this chapter to fill in that outline with more detail as we look at
some of the imperatives that are presented in Scripture.
Much of that detail has been referred to in the Bible texts
that have accompanied the chapters of this book.

## The Law and the Covenant

Israel was a people of the law. She heard directly from
God the Ten Commandments, or Ten Words, as the Hebrew is literally translated (Exodus 34:28). Moses recorded these and other directives by which Israel's people

1. R.E.O. White, *Biblical Ethics* (John Knox Press, 1980), p. 22.

were to conduct themselves. The law set Israel apart from her neighbors. The Hebrew people were a people consecrated to God, a people chosen to receive God's directives, a people bound in a covenant relationship with God. The law contained both civil and ceremonial directives. It guided both worship and daily life.

God said to the people of Israel before they received the law, "Now then, if you will indeed obey My voice and keep My covenant, then you shall be My own possession among all the peoples, for all the earth is Mine; and you shall be to Me a kingdom of priests and a holy nation" (Exodus 19:5, 6). The people responded, "All that the Lord has spoken we will do!" (Exodus 19:8). The law then was an expression of God's personal concern with His people; it was a code of divine sanction, not merely human wisdom; and it was intended to provide the Godlines by which a people of God's own possession might order themselves.

When asked as to the greatest of the commands, Jesus gave the essence of the law: "The foremost is, 'Hear, O Israel; the Lord our God is one Lord; and you shall love the Lord your God with all your heart, and with all your soul, and with all your mind, and with all your strength.' The second is this, 'You shall love your neighbor as yourself' " (Mark 12:29-31; Deuteronomy 6:4, 5).

The first four of the ten "words" from Sinai concern a person's relationship with God (Exodus 20:1-11). He is not to be trivialized, cheapened, or distorted by anything that may diminish His holiness, whether in thought, art, word, or worship. He is to be foremost in human minds and hearts. These four commandments set Israel uniquely apart from her neighbors. Her loyalty to one God only, her abhorrence of idolatry, her respect for the name and person of God, and her sacred day of rest marked her as unique in history.

The remaining six commandments concern a person's relationship with other people. The first emphasizes the importance God places on family relationships, the second the importance of human life, the third the importance of marital fidelity, the fourth the sanctity of personal property, the fifth the indispensable value of truth and integrity, and the sixth the importance of right attitude toward that which belongs to others. All of these person-to-person commandments are cited in some way or other in the New Testament (Matthew 5:21, 22, 27, 28; 15:19, 20; Mark 7:21-23; Romans 1:28-32; 13:9; 1 Corinthians 5:11; 6:9, 10; Ephesians 4:25, 28, 29; 5:3; 6:1-3; Colossians 3:2-5, 20, 21; 1 Peter 4:15; Revelation 21:8).

Israel's ritual, sacrificial, ceremonial law also set her apart from her neighbors. It was set down in meticulous detail that is very hard for us to appreciate. The rituals were to be observed without fail, but it is clear in God's revelation that ritual observance was to be no substitute for integrity, compassion, and obedience to God. Samuel thundered to King Saul, "Behold, to obey is better than sacrifice" (1 Samuel 15:22). As we read the Old Testament we are sometimes surprised at how the profoundest ethical teaching and the seemingly mundane matters of custom are put together (Leviticus 19:17-19). This underscores the fact that the Jews were to make no artificial distinction between religion, ritual, custom, and ethics. All were expressions of relationship with God.

Despite their separateness, the Jews were to have a special concern for foreigners and strangers in their midst. These were to be treated with the same respect, kindness, and consideration that one Jew would show to another (Leviticus 24:22). The poor, handicapped, and powerless were to be protected (Leviticus 19:13-18). There was special consideration for the needy and the stranger. At harvest time the farmer was not to glean a field or to reap the corners of it. A little grain and fruit must be left so the needy might gather food for themselves (Leviticus 19:9, 10; Deuteronomy 24:19-22). Thus the "welfare" plan required them to work.

God's concern extended to every aspect of a man's business, especially his weights and measures. "A just balance and scales belong to the Lord; all the weights of the bag are His concern" (Proverbs 16:11). As Barclay noted, "Here is the God not only of the sanctuary and the church, but of the counter and the shop floor. The weighing out of the housewife's order and the measuring of the customer's request become an act of worship for the Jew."[2]

God was concerned that a poor man have his cloak for warmth in the night (Exodus 22:26, 27; Deuteronomy 24:12, 13). God cared when a man got paid. He was to receive his wages each day (Deuteronomy 24:14, 15; Malachi 3:5). Widows and orphans were to be treated with justice and kindness.

While slavery was allowed, a servant, if he chose to do so, could go free after six years of service, without having to pay any compensation (Exodus 21:2-6). Not only this, but the master was generously to send him on his way with sheep, grain, and wine (Deuteronomy 15:12-18).

The Jew was to come to the aid of an animal that collapsed, even if it belonged to an enemy (Exodus 23:5; Deuteronomy 22:4). Animals, like people, rested on the Sabbath Day (Exodus 20:10). Lost property and strayed animals were to be returned to their owners (Deuteronomy 22:1-3). When constructing a new house, the Jew was to make a railing for his roof so that no one might fall from it (Deuteronomy 22:8). Even the mother bird sitting on her eggs was to be given special consideration (Deuteronomy 22:6, 7). Not only did the Jews rest on the seventh day, but they allowed their land to rest every seventh year (Leviticus 25:2-7).

A newly-married husband was to be exempt for a year from military service and any other duty that would take him away from home (Deuteronomy 24:5).

2. William Barclay, *Ethics in a Permissive Society* (Harper & Row, Publishers, Inc.), p. 24.

This brief sampling of Old Testament law underlines for us the fact that Biblical morality is characterized by concern, thoughtfulness, empathy, justice, honesty, kindness, impartiality, mercy, and respect for God and man.

## Jesus and the New Testament

We find the same basic elements in the New Testament. Concern and involvement are at the heart of Christian morality. The Christian is not merely to avoid evil. He aggressively is to seek the good (Matthew 7:12). In His Sermon on the Mount, Jesus began with a careful delineation of those beautiful attitudes that bring God's blessings to life. He made it clear that He came not to abolish the law and the prophets but to fulfill them. In a time that overly delighted in external obedience, He called for a return to the spirit of God's commandments. He examined not only the actions that the law prohibited, but the attitudes that lie behind the actions. He called for an attitude of reconciliation rather than retribution, giving rather than getting, loving rather than loathing, humility rather than hypocrisy, pardon rather than punishment, secrecy rather than show, awareness rather than anxiety, trust rather than tension, justice rather than judgment, prayer rather than power, involvement rather than indifference, character rather than conformity, goodness rather than gullibility, and righteousness rather than rhetoric.

Much of His ethical teaching came in the form of stories. The emphasis of Jesus and His apostles was not so much on rules as on the totality of life in God. One way to avoid the difficulties of legalism is to teach in paradoxes and parables. These force us not so much to conform to prescribed rules as to struggle, with fear and trembling, to apply the spirit of the teaching to our individual decisions. The parable of the good Samaritan indicts us whenever we are tempted to put religious duties or personal involvement above concern for the immediate needs of others. The parable of the prodigal son indicates God's loving, forgiving nature and underlines His joy at the repentance of a sinner.

It is not so much the content of Jesus' ethical teaching that sets Him apart from all other moralists. It is the fact that He himself perfectly embodied all that He taught. In Him there is no inconsistency between word and action. He is therefore our standard for human conduct, the model for our imitation (Ephesians 4:15). To do the right is to take on the character of Jesus. He is the way, the truth, the life (John 14:6).

Jesus expressed perfect love in His death on the cross (John 15:13). He was abused, but did not retaliate (1 Peter 2:19-23). He prayed for those who nailed Him to the cross (Luke 23:34). Though He was God's own Son, He became the servant of others (John 13:3-17). His life was lived in complete conformity with God's will (Matthew 26:39).

The writings of Paul and other New Testament writers center on Jesus and on the life-style that is to be lived in Christ. We are to love our neighbors as ourselves (Galatians 5:14). Our freedom in Christ is not to be used as an excuse for license, but as an opportunity for love and service to one another. The deeds of the flesh—immorality, impurity, sensuality, idolatry, sorcery, enmities, strife, jealousy, outbursts of anger, disputes, dissensions, factions, envyings, drunkenness, and carousings—are to be put to death (Galatians 5:14-21). In their place is to be the fruit of the Spirit—love, joy, peace, patience, kindness, goodness, faithfulness, gentleness, and self-control (Galatians 5:22, 23). The church is to be a loving, caring, comforting community (Galatians 6:1-6).

Christians are those who in Christ put on a new self "which in the likeness of God has been created in righteousness and holiness of the truth" (Ephesians 4:24). They are to be truthful, peaceable, honest, hard-working, generous to those in need, mindful of their words, kind, tenderhearted, and forgiving (Ephesians 4:25-32). In short, they are to be imitators of God (Ephesians 5:1). There is to be no immorality, greed, filthy talk, coarse jesting, impurity, or idolatry. Instead of these there should always be love, goodness, righteousness, and truth (Ephesians 5:2-10).

Christians are to be circumspect in the use of time, seeking to know the will of the Lord (Ephesians 5:16). They are to be subject to one another. Wives are to be subject to their husbands, and husbands are to love their wives. Children are to obey their parents; parents are to be considerate of their children. Slaves are to be obedient to their masters, rendering their service to God, not to men; masters are to be considerate of their slaves (Ephesians 5:20—6:9).

Peter called upon Christians to be exemplary citizens (1 Peter 2:13-15). "Honor all men; love the brotherhood, fear God, honor the king," he wrote (1 Peter 2:17), though perhaps even then Emperor Nero was massacring the Christians. Servants are to give loyal service even to harsh masters. Wives are to be submissive, chaste, respectful of their husbands; husbands are to be understanding and respectful of their wives. "To sum up," he wrote, "let all be harmonious, sympathetic, brotherly, kind-hearted, and humble in spirit; not returning evil for evil, or insult for insult, but giving a blessing instead; for you were called for the very purpose that you might inherit a blessing" (1 Peter 3:8, 9).

James called on men and women to control their anger (James 1:19, 20) and to control their tongues (James 1:26). Pure religion, to James, is to visit orphans and widows and to keep from being stained by the world (James 1:27). Christians are to show impartiality, to be merciful, and actively to be involved in meeting human needs (James 2). They are to be gentle, unselfish, magnanimous, pure, peaceable, reasonable, unwavering, and genuine (James 3:13-18).

James saw an internal war as the source of evil in human life. People seem to continually seek the wrong things. They lust, envy, fight, and quarrel. Their eyes are on themselves rather than on God. In their arrogance, they oppose God and He opposes them. Such people think they are totally independent of God, but in reality not even their lives are truly theirs. Only when a man completely humbles himself and seeks God can he begin to receive God's favor. Life must be lived with consciousness that judgment is at hand and that God will not ignore the selfish advantage that has been taken of others (James 4:1—5:9).

John expanded on James' theme that the Christian is to keep himself unstained by the world. John wrote, ''Do not love the world, nor the things in the world. If any one loves the world, the love of the Father is not in him. For all that is in the world, the lust of the flesh and the lust of the eyes and the boastful pride of life, is not from the Father, but is from the world. And the world is passing away, and also its lusts; but the one who does the will of God abides forever (1 John 2:15-17). These three—the lust of the flesh, the lust of the eyes, and the boastful pride of life—are the prime temptation points of human life. The lust of the flesh has to do with our relationships with our physical bodies. How do we use our bodies? Who is in control of them? To what extent do we live on the basis of our drives and appetites? The lust of the eyes has to do with our relationship with material things. How do we use our personal resources? How important are things to us? Do we look only at the tangible? The boastful pride of life has to do with who will be preeminent in our lives—God or ourselves. It has to do with our world view. Is man the center or is God the center? Is God's will to be followed, or our will? Hedonism, materialism, and naturalism are all modern expressions of these things of the world. All of these things pass away. Death removes us from our material acquisitions, and it removes us from our physical pleasures. *But the one who does the will of God abides forever.*

We have noted in previous chapters that many moderns have ruled God out of their consideration of right and wrong. They consider man the only significant reality. They have boasted of their liberation from Biblical morality, but their boasted freedom is nothing but bondage to sin (2 Peter 2:18, 19). God, however, remains at the center of the universe. His Word offers man's only true compass. We have considered only a brief sampling of His revelation. It remains for each of us to search that Word diligently for the way of life. He wants not so much the control of our actions as the lordship of our lives.

# MORAL PROBLEMS

*Please read Colossians 3:1—4:6.*

The Bible clearly distinguishes good actions from bad ones. It also agrees that there are times when, on the "lesser evil" principle, it may regrettably be *right* to do something bad, because there is no better alternative. But in these cases the bad does not automatically become *good* because it is the right thing to do in the circumstances.[1]

The Bible conveys its teachings for human behavior by means of personal examples (e.g. Abraham), direct commandments (e.g. the Old Testament law code), general principles (e.g. Paul's teaching about concern for the weaker brother), parables (e.g. the good Samaritan), and wise maxims (e.g. the book of Proverbs). Sometimes an attempt is made to draw all these together into a concise guidebook for human conduct. That which is alluded to in the book of Proverbs is put together with Old Testament laws and combined with New Testament teachings as if

1. David Field, *Free to Do Right* (InterVarsity Press 1973), p. 23.

all were on the same footing. Since the Old Testament is larger, contains much more personal history, records many more laws, and includes a whole book of maxims, this approach tends to diminish the importance of the New Testament. The Old Testament, while enlightening and useful, is not the code-book of laws for Christian behavior. The Christian must look especially to the New Testament for guidance in his actions.

## The Center of Gravity

Some Christians suggest that whatever of the Old Testament is not directly rescinded in the New Testament is still binding on the Christian under the New Covenant. Others suggest that only that which is specifically repeated in the New is binding, all the rest having been done away. These are large and difficult questions, but it should be said emphatically that the New Testament is God's completed revelation and that it supersedes the Old Testament as our rule of faith and conduct (Hebrews 8:6-13). Just as British common law serves as the background for American law, the Old Testament provides the roots for the New Testament. And just as Americans are not bound directy to British law, so the Christian is not bound to the Old Testament regulations. It is to the New Covenant that the Christian must look as he judges his responsibilities, his goals, his attitudes and his conduct.

## Silences

As Christians we must deal with some areas where the Bible is apparently silent. Some people argue that silences are virtually prohibitions, while others argue that silences indicate areas of free choice. This underscores the dubious nature of arguments from silence. We must search the Scriptures for principles that will apply to new situations as they arise, but we also must be careful not to presume to speak with Biblical authority in areas where the Bible is silent. Further, we should beware of the cultist who capitalizes on the ambiguities and silences of Scripture to construct his own idiosyncratic system to "unlock" the Bible.

## Principles and Applications

The Bible, as we have noted, is not a legal codebook, laying down rules and precedents for every conceivable situation that can possibly arise in human behavior. Such a book would be hopelessly technical, impossibly large, and incredibly dull. By giving general, overall principles that can be applied in many different situations and in many different cultures, the Bible remains constantly contemporaneous.

In a sense the Bible is like the American Constitution, sketching out large areas of responsibility and freedom; but it must be interpreted in individual cases as they arise. It is here that many of our problems occur. It is clear, for instance, that murder is wrong. But is abortion always murder? Is killing in self-defense murder? Is killing in war murder? Is capital punishment murder? Is euthanasia murder? Is unplugging a life-support machine on a terminally-ill patient murder? That murder is wrong, all agree; but whether a certain action can properly be defined within that category is a question that is not easily settled.

## Casuistry and Situationism

There are at least two ways to deal with the problem of applying general laws to particular cases. One is to construct an elaborate system of laws and definitions. This is the approach of the *casuist,* whose solution is to amplify the commandments of the Bible. He constructs a whole system of by-laws designed to encompass every conceivable set of circumstances. The attempt is made to legislate for every imaginable situation of life. We have referred earlier to the work of the Pharisees in this regard.

Their Sabbath rules were the result of long deliberation. In those rules they tried to spell out what one could do for a sore throat on the Sabbath and what he was allowed to do if a wall fell and covered up his neighbor. This was the way of the Jesuits in the seventeenth century and of some religious systematizers of today. The problem with this approach is obvious. It leads to a spirit of legalism and hair-splitting that at length encrusts the spirit of Biblical injunctions with such a load of behavioral barnacles that it can no longer live. Eventually the lawyers have so obliterated the spirit of the law that they can devise acceptable reasons for breaking it outright.

The situationist, as we noted earlier, takes the opposite approach. He attempts to condense the commandments into one overriding principle. Joseph Fletcher chose love. Thus all is made subservient to love; whatever does not serve love, as it is interpreted, is to be scrapped. As to abortion, premarital sex, self-defense, war, capital punishment, and active and passive euthanasia, the situationist's answer is, "It all depends." He wants only to know how love will be served in each instance. Before long, however, he too has laid waste the original command by his exceptions to it.

The casuist, then, tries to fill in the gaps of Biblical revelation with his own interpretations, judgments, and applications. The situationist, in the name of one high absolute, cuts himself loose from Biblical commandments, except as they may serve some advisory role toward love. The casuist is concerned with the letter of the law; the situationist with the spirit. But either may finally violate the law.

We must recognize that treading the path between these extremes may be difficult. We may, like the casuist, feel the need to define life as it relates to the fetus in our discussions of abortion. And we may, like the situationist, have occasions where we appeal to a hierarchy of values when absolutes conflict. But we must be careful that we do not undercut, in either spirit or letter, the whole counsel of God as revealed in the Bible.

## Absolutes in Conflict

While it is true that sometimes Biblical principles and commandments collide with one another, generally they do not. The fact that ethical dilemmas occur in *abnormal* situations should not serve as an excuse for ignoring God's directives in *normal* situations. Nevertheless, we are sometimes faced with situations where it seems that to be faithful to one Biblical principle is to violate another.

It is easy to think of cases of this kind. Is a husband right in breaking the speed limit (duty to law and government) in order to get his wife to the hospital for an emergency operation (duty to life and wife)? The answer to that seems pretty obvious to most of us, for we tend to be pretty casual about speed limits even in ordinary circumstances. But what if the husband's speed causes an accident in which his wife and five other people are killed? In that case we might return to a judgment based on duty to law.

What about a teen-ager who desires to become a Christian, but his parents forbid his being baptized, going to church, and reading the Bible? What is he to do? The Bible clearly directs him to be obedient to his parents (Colossians 3:20); but it also tells him that anyone who loves father or mother more than Jesus is not worthy of Him (Matthew 10:37). Some Christian teachers advise that he should be obedient to his parents, for that is his prime obligation. He should pray and wait for God to change their hearts. His example of obedience will, it is said, open the way to his sharing his faith with his parents and lead to their eventual conversion. To disobey parents is to rebel against God-given parental authority and to alienate them from himself, from his church, and from his Christ. Other teachers encourage the young man to step out in faith, giving up all if necessary, to follow Jesus. Loyalty to God must take precedence over loyalty to parents. He must be prepared to endure persecution from his parents as a loyal follower of Christ.

One could wish that such dilemmas would never occur, and in a less sin-stained world there would be far fewer. Solutions and judgments are not simple. Often we must act in awareness of our limited understanding. It is somewhat comforting to note that a number of people in the Bible faced similar dilemmas. Abraham must certainly have felt the tension of son-love and God-love in his obedience to God's command to sacrifice his son Isaac (Genesis 22:1-19; Hebrews 11:17-19). Peter must certainly have felt the tension between truth and his desire to be near Jesus during the agonizing hour of His trial before the high priest (Matthew 26:69-75). Rahab faced a similar moral dilemma when helping the Hebrew spies (Joshua 2:1-7, Hebrews 11:31, James 2:25). The Hebrew midwives had to decide whether to obey God or the king (Exodus 1:15-21), as did Daniel (Daniel 6) and his friends (Daniel 3). Each of these instances may be studied carefully for insight into situations of conflicting ethical principles.

The dilemma most often cited in discussions of this kind is the one that faced Rahab—lying to save life. Three basic answers are given by those who believe in absolute, normative standards of conduct: (1) You should tell the truth regardless of the consequencs. (2) You should lie, without remorse, recognizing that you have a moral obligation to value life over truth. (3) You should lie, recognizing that lying, while excusable in this instance, is the lesser of two evils and a wrong requiring repentance.

Those holding the first view contend that we should never choose evil to bring about good (Romans 3:8). Our duty is to be true to the demands of the law and to let God take care of the consequences. We may refuse to say anything at all, of course. In some cases that may offer a way out of the dilemma. But in other cases silence may be an admission that can lead to death, as with a Nazi's insistent question as to whether Jews were hiding in a certain house. Regardless of outcome, this position sees its primary responsibility as the preserving of the moral code. It is felt that God will not allow evil to result from an action on our part that is intrinsically good. The problem with this view is that it seems insensitive and deterministic, as well as an evasion of personal responsibility to intervene to bring the most possible good from a bad situation. This view also assumes that all moral principles and commandments are of equal standing and that there is no gradation of responsibility, an assumption that seems to run counter to the teaching of Jesus (John 19:11).

The second position recognizes that some obligations are higher than others and that we are responsible for serving the highest good. This means the construction of some sort of hierarchy of obligation in which the lower always gives way to the higher. Thus truth-telling is binding in all cases but those in which it must give way to a higher responsibility. In this view, there is no sin involved in making the choice to break a lower duty for the sake of a higher. It is the morally right thing to do. One problem with this position is the difficulty in constructing a hierarchy that is free from arbitrariness and self-interest. Sometimes it is not clear how the Bible absolutes rank or what general principles should govern our hierarchy. Rather than face martyrdom, for instance, we might decide that renunciation of our faith is only a lie and of less importance than life. This position tends toward the undercutting of Biblical authority by allowing Biblical absolutes to be systematically overridden without a sense of guilt.

The person holding the third view must also have in mind a hierarchy, for he chooses the lesser of two evils. Even if his choice is the best of the options available to him, he must recognize his violation of duty as sin. He must repent of it before God. He recognizes the absolute standard of the law, but he realizes that he acts within a less-than-perfect world. He is forced into a decision that is necessary, but nevertheless evil. In contrast to the second position, this position interprets the best action available, if it violates a Christian duty, as a sin rather than a positive good.

All of these positions have been advocated by dedicated Christian thinkers. Each has its strengths and its weaknesses. But it seems to me that the third position comes closest to reconciling man's need to be involved for good in a defective world and his need to honor with his heart, soul, and mind the commands of God.

One possible solution to these difficulties is to withdraw as much as possible from human affairs. Many Christians do not wish to be involved in politics because it requires the frequent weighing of issues that cannot be easily classified. But if we leave that area to those who give homage to no absolute moral standards, do we not contribute to the moral decay of our nation?

It is well that, as we close this discussion of thorny and difficult matters, we look carefully at Paul's instructions to the Colossians (3:1—4:6). He calls on Christians to seek those things which are above. As Christians we must look beyond our immediate advantage or some temporary expediency to the will and purpose of God. We are to put aside the sins of the old self and be renewed in true knowledge by Christ. We are to be compassionate, kind, humble, gentle, patient, forgiving, and loving. The peace of Christ occupies our hearts and we are filled with thanksgiving. We give constant attention to the Word of God, and our every action is done in the name of Jesus. Love, loyalty, obedience, understanding, and sincerity rule in our lives—lives that are lived heartily, not hesitantly or timidly, as unto the Lord. It is Christ who will judge all without partiality. Our speech is to be graceful and full of God's wisdom. Wisdom and grace come through diligence in prayer and thanksgiving.

As we face the moral dilemmas of our lives, we should be reminded that we need not a system but a Savior. Diligent prayer will do more to resolve our moral dilemmas than hours of learned debate.

# MORAL POWER

*Please read Romans 6:12-23; 7:15-25; Philippians 2:3-16.*

Grace and peace be multiplied to you in the knowledge of God and of Jesus our Lord; seeing that His divine power has granted to us everything pertaining to life and godliness, through the true knowledge of Him who called us by His own glory and excellence. For by these He has granted to us His precious and magnificent promises, in order that by them you might become partakers of the divine nature, having escaped the corruption that is in the world by lust. Now for this very reason also, applying all diligence, in your faith supply moral excellence, and in your moral excellence, knowledge; and in your knowledge, self-control, and in your self-control, perseverance, and in your perseverance, godliness; and in your godliness, brotherly kindness, and in your brotherly kindness, Christian love.[1]

---

1. 2 Peter 1:2-7.

For all our discussion about knowing the good, mankind's primary problem is not so much *knowing* what is right as *doing* what is right. For all our variations of philosophy, world view, and basic assumptions, we have, as C. S. Lewis well pointed out, amazing unanimity in regard to right and wrong. What we lack, however, is the incentive and the power to do the good we know we ought to do.

## Incentive

The Bible talks a great deal about reward and punishment. The faithful, the righteous, the holy are promised God's blessing. The evil, the disobedient, the rebellious are promised God's condemnation and punishment.

There are those who would suggest that such appeals to self-interest are somehow beneath God. We should, they assert, be good for goodness' sake, not for Heaven's sake.

Yet God, who *created* human nature, *knows* human nature. God knows that man has a desire for significance; He made him that way. There is nothing so grating to humankind as that which is useless, purposeless, and unnecessary. God's Word gives us insight into the true significance of our lives. We are given a glimpse into eternity in order that we may have incentive to view life in terms of eternal consequences.

Further, our spirits demand justice. God's revelation of righteous judgment assures us that there will someday be a righting of the wrongs that have gone unrighted in human history.

## The Great Civil War

Love, duty, reverence, hope, faith—all of these unite to provide incentive for us to do the right that we know we ought to do. But many times we find ourselves, like Paul, crying out, "For that which I am doing, I do not understand; for I am not practicing what I would like to do, but I am doing the very thing I hate (Romans 7:15). Paul verbalized the seemingly endless conflict we so often feel. It seems as if a great civil war is raging within us, and we continually find ourselves incapable of responding to the good. We are in bondage to sin, and it has taken rule over us. We confess, like Paul, "For the good that I wish, I do not do; but I practice the very evil that I do not wish" (Romans 7:19).

This has been the great dilemma of moral philosophy throughout the ages. It is the gap between normative and descriptive ethics. It is the difference between the ethics we give lip service to and that which we actually practice. We find ourselves despising our evil and self-destructive actions, but we turn right around and do them again and again. We make our resolutions. We determine by sheer willpower to overcome our sinful habits. But soon we are back in the old ruinous rut, discouraged, guilty, and defeated. What force is powerful enough to break us out of this sorrowful cycle?

To Paul, it was like a battle between his mind and his body—a battle that his mind was losing (Romans 7:22, 23). He, like us, cried out, "Wretched man that I am! Who will set me free from the body of this death?" (Romans 7:24).

The answer to this moral dilemma is Jesus Christ. From the thankful recesses of his joyful heart, Paul shouted out, "Thanks be to God through Jesus Christ our Lord!" (Romans 7:25).

## The Law and Grace

Just how does Jesus Christ enter into man's moral dilemma? Paul discusses this at length in his letters to the Romans and to the Galatians. One of his first assumptions is that no man can claim to live up perfectly to the law of God (Galatians 3:10, 11; Romans 3:23). And the law itself asserts, "Cursed is he who does not confirm the words of this law by doing them" (Deuteronomy 27:26).

There are many in our day who say, "I'm really not much interested in religion; I just try to live by the Ten Commandments." Paul would say, I think, "Beware then, for if you live by them you will be judged by them. And no one can claim to stand uncondemned by the law."

The law of God, as recorded in the Bible, serves to define wrongdoing in order that we may identify it and flee from it. But it provides us no power actually to overcome wrongdoing. To use a medical analogy, the law diagnoses sin, but has no cure for it. Further, the law, ironically, works against itself in that by its very prohibitions it may awaken in us a desire for disobedience Romans 7:8). We seem almost to take delight in doing those things that are prohibited. The result of the law is to expose our weakness, our sinfulness, and our need to throw ourselves upon the mercy and grace of God. As William Barclay puts it, "The law shows us our own helplessness, convinces us of our own insufficiency, and in the end compels us to admit that the only thing which can save us is not this impossible obedience to the law but the grace of God."[2]

The realization that we are sinners, that we can never stand before God on the basis of our own righteousness or our good works, is a necessary first step toward our understanding of God's loving provision for man. Paul wrote, "Nevertheless knowing that a man is not justified by the works of the Law but through faith in Christ Jesus, even we have believed in Christ Jesus, that we may be justified by faith in Christ, and not by the works of the Law; since by the works of the Law shall no flesh be justified" (Galatians 2:16).

It is not by perfect obedience to the laws of God that we can hope to be righteous, but by faith in Jesus Christ. It is

2. From *THE LETTERS TO THE GALATIANS AND EPHESIANS*, Translated with Introductions and Interpretations by William Barclay. First published by The Saint Andrew Press. Published in the U.S.A. by The Westminster Press. Used by permission.

said of Abraham, who lived long before the Mosaic law was given, that he believed God and that his faith was reckoned to him as righteousness (Galatians 3:6; Romans 4:3). The Christian also lives by faith (Galatians 3:11).

The commandments brought all men under the condemnation of sin "that the promise by faith in Jesus Christ might be given to those who believe" (Galatians 3:22). The law functioned primarily to lead to Christ in order that mankind might be justified by faith (Galatians 3:24). It is not our goodness, our perfect ability to observe all the commandments of God, that makes us children of God. It is faith in Jesus Christ (Galatians 3:26). In baptism, the Christian clothes himself with Christ, unites himself with Christ, and submits himself to Christ (Galatians 3:27-29).

## Justification

We spoke earlier of righteousness. It is clear from Scripture and from our personal experience that none of us can claim to have lived perfectly righteous lives. But through our faith in Jesus Christ we enter into a relationship with Him whereby we are judged before God in light of Christ's righteousness rather than our own unrighteousness. The Scriptural term for this is *justification*.

Our sinfulness condemns us, but God's love in Christ treats us as if we were guiltless. Paul wrote, "There is therefore now no condemnation for those who are in Christ Jesus. For the law of the Spirit of life in Christ Jesus has set you free from the law of sin and of death. . . . And if Christ is in you, though the body is dead because of sin, yet the spirit is alive because of righteousness. . . . Who will bring a charge against God's elect? God is the one who justifies; who is the one who condemns? Christ Jesus is He who died, yes, rather who was raised, who is at the right hand of God, who also intercedes for us" (Romans 8:1-34). Justified by faith, we have peace with God through Jesus. Through faith in

Jesus we are introduced into God's grace and we joy in the hope of the glory of God (Romans 5:1, 2). We stand before God clothed in the righteousness of Jesus.

All this sounds very theological to our ears and seems somehow remote from the philosophical approach of the early part of the book. But herein is truth that touches all aspects of human behavior. The fact is that no one can stand before God on the basis of his own goodness. We are all utter failures in recognizing and doing the good and in shunning the evil. We may feel fairly comfortable about ourselves if we compare ourselves with others like ourselves. We may claim that we are no worse than average and that, for the most part, we try to ''do the right thing.'' But that is not nearly enough in the eyes of God, who is the ultimate judge of all human conduct. We must all cast ourselves on the mercy of God, through faith partake of the imputed righteousness that God's grace provides through Jesus Christ, and set ourselves upon a course of loving response to His Spirit.

Does all this mean then that we personally have no necessity to strive to obey God's commandments? Of course not. Paul wrote, ''What then? Shall we sin because we are not under law but under grace? May it never be! . . . But thanks be to God that though you were slaves of sin, you became obedient from the heart to that form of teaching to which you were committed, and having been freed from sin, you became slaves of righteousness'' (Romans 6:15-18).

Imperatives to right conduct leap from nearly every page of Scripture. God has created us with free will and with the ability to conform our wills to His. Paul urges the Christian to work out his salvation with fear and trembling (Philippians 2:12). This points to man's part in seeking to know and to do God's will. But Paul goes on to emphasize that God is a partner in this as well: ''For it is God who is at work in you, both to will and to work for His good pleasure'' (Philippians 2:13). God will help us to bring our recalcitrant wills into submission. He supplies both motive and motion to do the right when we open up our hearts to the power and saving work of Jesus Christ.

## The Holy Spirit

The Holy Spirit is an enabler in the life of the Christian as he seeks to do the good. Paul wrote, "But if the Spirit of Him who raised Jesus from the dead dwells in you, He who raised Christ Jesus from the dead will also give life to your mortal bodies through His Spirit who indwells you. So then, brethren, we are under obligation, not to the flesh, to live according to the flesh—for if you are living according to the flesh, you must die; but if by the Spirit you are putting to death the deeds of the body, you will live. For all who are being led by the Spirit of God, these are sons of God" (Romans 8:11-14). The Spirit helps in our weakness and assists in our prayers (Romans 8:26, 27). The Spirit enabled Paul to know the deep things of God (1 Corinthians 2:10-12). The Spirit is in conflict with the deeds of the flesh (Galatians 5:16-23). A person reaps what he sows. If he sows to the Spirit he will reap from the Spirit eternal life (Galatians 6:8). Paul wrote to Titus, "He saved us, not on the basis of deeds which we have done in righteousness, but according to His mercy, by the washing of regeneration and renewing by the Holy Spirit, whom He poured out upon us richly through Jesus Christ our Savior, that being justified by His grace we might be made heirs according to the hope of eternal life" (Titus 3:5-7). God does not leave us unaided to do the right which He commands.

## God's Provision

God motivates us through His example of love, through the model of Jesus, and through the promise of eternal life. When we fail, He forgives us and accepts us through grace. He has provided, through Jesus, if we respond to Him in faith, the righteousness we lack. We are clothed in

Christ's righteousness and acquitted before the judgment bar of God. Through faith and obedience we receive the indwelling of the Holy Spirit to enable us to understand and to do God's revealed will. As we express our love to God in obedience to His commands, He is at work in our spirits to prompt us to the right and to enable us to do the right.

There are those who suggest that this act of putting to death the sinfulness of the flesh is sudden and complete at the moment of conversion. Yet Scripture leads me to believe that it is a continuing process that will go on as long as we dwell in our mortal bodies. We cannot completely escape our humanity, with its limited knowledge, its limited powers, its sin-tainted nature. But we can live in hope, knowing that if we set our feet on God's path, if we believe in Jesus Christ and trust Him, and if we make obedience to the expressed will of God our highest aim, we have nothing to fear from our loving Father.

Let us retrace, for a moment, the path we have taken through the morality maze. In the beginning chapters we examined the moral malaise of our time. We looked at the futility of any view of moral conduct that does not ground itself in the revelation of God. We saw that a man-centered ethic becomes a man-destroying ethic. We saw that any ethical structure that contradicts God's commands is doomed to inconsistency and perversion. Having run into the cul-de-sac of man-centered thinking, we reoriented ourselves by the revelation of God. In the Bible we found God's identification of the good, the true, and the right. We examined some of the Bible's teaching about human conduct, conduct toward God and toward man. We struggled with the practical application of God's commands in difficult situations. Finally, we focused on Christ, God's loving provision to free man from his sinful and estranged condition.

It is hoped that our walk through the morality maze has not been merely an academic pursuit. Our goal has not been merely to play with a puzzle. It has been to point to a person, Jesus Christ, who alone gives meaning, purpose, and hope to life. "Now the God of peace, who brought up from the dead the great Shepherd of the sheep through the blood of the eternal covenant, even Jesus our Lord, equip you in every good thing to do His will, working in us that which is pleasing in His sight, through Jesus Christ; to whom be the glory forever and ever. Amen" (Hebrews 13:20, 21).